The Sporting World of
R. S. Surtees

The Sporting World of
R. S. SURTEES

JOHN WELCOME

Oxford New York

OXFORD UNIVERSITY PRESS

Oxford University Press, Walton Street, Oxford OX2 6DP

London Glasgow New York Toronto
Delhi Bombay Calcutta Madras Karachi
Kuala Lumpur Singapore Hong Kong Tokyo
Nairobi Dar es Salaam Cape Town
Melbourne Auckland

and associate companies in
Beirut Berlin Ibadan Mexico City

First published 1982.   Reprinted 1982

British Library Cataloguing in Publication Data
Welcome, John
The sporting world of R.S. Surtees.
1. Surtees, Robert Smith 2. Authors, English
—19th century—Biography
I. Title
823'.8   PR5499.S4
ISBN 0-19-211766-1

Printed and bound in Great Britain by
Robert Hartnoll Ltd., Bodmin, Cornwall

308578

Acknowledgements

Mr E. D. Cuming, the discoverer of the Surtees manuscripts, published these with a commentary in 1924. This was followed by Mr Frederick Watson's 'critical study' in 1933 and Mr Leo Cooper's literary appraisal of 1952. Nothing relating to Surtees in book form has been published since then and the authors of these three works would not, it seems reasonable to assume, have claimed them as biographies. Surtees is far from forgotten, especially amongst sporting people, and there is at the time of writing talk of forming a Surtees Society. This seemed an appropriate time therefore to attempt a comprehensive life, placing him in the sporting, literary, and social context of his time.

Although essentially a private person much of him can be deduced from the books, parts of which are clearly autobiographical, and modern photostating facilities have provided means of exploring the pages of the many magazines which proliferated during Surtees's writing life which research has, amongst other things, thrown new light on the stormy relations between Nimrod and Surtees, the two men who dominated sporting literature in the first half of the nineteenth century.

It is necessary to thank all those, librarians and others, who have given their assistance, especially the Librarian of the London Library who, as always, has been a tower of strength in searching for and obtaining out of print books which otherwise could not have been consulted. Acknowledgement must also be made to Constable Publishers for permission to quote from Michael Sadleir, *Trollope: A Commentary*; to J. M. Dent & Sons Ltd for words from G. K. Chesterton's Introduction to Charles Dickens, *The Pickwick Papers* (Everyman's Library); to A. P. Watt Ltd., for extracts from A. P. Herbert, *Tantivy Towers* (Methuen, 1931), and from Rudyard Kipling, *My Son's Wife* from *A Diversity of Creatures* (Macmillan, 1917); and to Humphrey Lyttelton for permission to quote from a letter from his father to Sir Rupert Hart-Davis in the *Lyttelton—Hart–Davis Letters*, Vol. 2 (John Murray).

Contents

Illustrations

CHAPTER ONE

Opening Days

'I NEVER push myself an inch forward but I damned well see I'm never pushed an inch back.'[1] These words—one of the few self-revelatory remarks he ever made—contain many of the keys to the strange and contradictory character of the greatest writer of sporting fiction in English literature.

He was a north-country squire, dour, reticent, taciturn, and of an unforgiving frame of mind. He was touchy and quarrelsome, envious of success in others and sometimes spiteful in expressing this envy. Yet he was also an upright man and a firm friend who measured people at their worth or more often their worthlessness with an accurate and unsparing eye, and sought for truth with a vision unclouded by sentimentality or self-deception. His exceptional powers of observation and recall, his ear for colloquial dialogue and ability to write hard prose and coin a telling phrase, enabled him to create in his books a galaxy of characters unique in English fiction, and one immortal.

Robert Smith Surtees was born on 17 May 1805 and baptized on 20 August 1806. He was the second son of Anthony Surtees of Hamsterley Hall, County Durham and one of a large family of nine, several of whom died young. The Surtees were an old family. They traced their origins back to the tenth century and claimed that their name came from the River Tees and was a corruption of the words Super Tysam. The family had owned property in County Durham for generations and Robert's father, Anthony, bought Hamsterley Hall, where Robert grew up, early in the nineteenth century from the executors of Robert Swinburne. He retained ownership of his former holding at Milkenwellburn House,

1

however, where his father, grandfather, and great-grandfather had all kept and hunted hounds. Anthony followed their tradition and indeed improved on it for he kept two packs, one of foxhounds and one of harriers, which he divided between his two residences. Robert, the future author, was therefore born into a sporting family, early entered to fox-hunting and reared in its science and traditions.

The country over which Anthony Surtees and his neighbour, Ralph Lambton hunted was a rough one, and there was little of the smart or fashionable about either hunt. The fields which followed the packs consisted of a few local gentry and tenant farmers conspicuous more for their workmanlike appearance than smartness of turnout. There was little jumping and nothing to attract 'fashionables' from other countries. It was the sort of country where was practised the true science of venery of which Anthony Surtees and Ralph Lambton, especially the latter, were masters. Ralph Lambton was to become Surtees's beau ideal of a man, a Master of Foxhounds and a huntsman for whom Surtees conceived a hero-worship most unusual for one of his cynical temperament.

Lambton came from a Durham family almost as old as the Surtees, their estates having been acquired at the time of the Norman Conquest. He was the second son of General Lambton and Lady Susan Lyon and kinsman to the Earls of Durham. 'Ralph Lambton', Surtees wrote later, 'was indeed a model master and a model man—just the sort of character for youth to be taught to look up to as a perfect specimen of a highly polished English gentleman—so courteous, so considerate, so alive to all the little delicacies by which pleasure is conferred or pain excited; above all so truly honourable in his conduct, and sincere and faithful in his friendships. . . . He never forgot anything or anybody, and had a wonderful memory for facts. He had the eye of an eagle for detecting a fault, and the air of a Grandison in reproving one.' And he gives as an example of Lambton's mild yet effective way of controlling his field his reproof to one thruster pressing his hounds too hard at a check: 'Hold hard, sir! *Venus has it under*

2

your horse's feet!' 'Still', Surtees goes on to say, 'Mr Ralph could give it a good deal harder than that when occasion required, when his objurgations were emphatic and truly original.'[2]

Those 'original objurgations' may well have been the inspiration for Lord Scamperdale's frequent, fluent, and damnatory explosions of wrath which he poured forth on the offending head of Mr Soapey Sponge for overriding hounds and other similar sins much later on, for Surtees stored everything away in his amazing memory and never let a joke, a phrase, or an experience go past him:

'Thank you, Mr Brown Boots! . . . Hang'd obleged to you, Mr Brown Boots! D—n *you*, Mr Brown Boots! . . . you've lost us our fox, sir—*yes*, sir—lost us our fox, sir. D'ye call that nothin', sir? If you don't, *I* do, you perpendicular-looking Puseyite pig-jobber! By Jove! you think because I'm a lord, and can't swear, or use coarse language, that you may do what you like—but I'll take my hounds home, sir—yes, sir, I'll take my hounds home, sir.'

Mr Sponge's Sporting Tour, Chapter 20

Surely there are echoes here of those 'original objurgations' and 'giving it a good deal harder when required'?

Ralph Lambton was to him and always remained the perfect example of a sportsman and a gentleman. The all but fulsome praise bestowed upon him is unique where Surtees's writings and opinions are concerned and demonstrates the impact Ralph Lambton's charm and character had upon him. For Surtees looked on humanity with a cold and unsparing eye and was setting this down towards the end of his life when age and experience might have been expected to have tempered the enthusiasm of youth.

Little is known of Surtees's childhood. At an early age he was packed off to Ovingham School seven miles distant from Hamsterley Hall. There appears to have been no intention to send him to Eton or one of the more fashionable southern schools, and he remained at Ovingham until he was thirteen when he was sent to Durham Grammar School. Here he stayed for only a year after which time he was held to have completed his education and was removed by his parents.

Ovingham and Durham appear to have been little different from the usual run of schools of the time. They were tough and primitive but there seems to have been no bullying for Surtees has left a fragmentary account of his school-days and had he suffered any brutalities he was not someone to overlook them. What he does record, however, is that 'The school [Ovingham] was kept by the Rev James Birkett, who combined the business of schoolmaster with that of gardener, farmer, and walking-stick maker. He had the most ludicrous propensity for making and hoarding up walking-sticks that ever was heard of. He could not see or hear of a promising sapling but he would be at it . . .'[3] Even at that early age the young Surtees was storing away impressions and observations for future use and in due course Mr Birkett became Mr Jogglebury Crowdey in *Mr Sponge's Sporting Tour* published over forty years later.

The holidays from school were spent at Hamsterley in the active enjoyment of field sports—fishing, hunting, and shooting in due season. An accident with his gun during this time, the details of which have gone unrecorded, lessened his interest in shooting and he was never a keen shot afterwards though he would go out with the guns and occasionally enjoy a day with his dogs. He once sent Thackeray a present of a grouse and his lack of enthusiasm for shooting as a sport did not prevent him including shooting scenes in his novels nor from ensuring that they were technically accurate and correct.

From childhood onwards his real love was for hunting. 'All time is lost wot is not spent in huntin'' he made Mr Jorrocks say and this, like many other of Mr Jorrocks's sentiments, echoed exactly those of his creator. As well as following his father's and Mr Lambton's foxhounds he was constantly out with Mr Surtees's harriers. This gave him an insight into the sport and science of hare-hunting, and though he was to make Mr Jorrocks quote with appreciation 'How poor the triumph o'er the timid hare', he was constantly to express interest in and sympathy with those who hunted harriers at a time when they were much looked down upon by fox-hunters.

In the first quarter of the nineteenth century second sons of the squirearchy were of little account and Surtees was no exception. The only occupations or professions considered suitable for them were the Army, the Church, the law, and possibly, medicine, in that descending order or, for the quite hopeless, a quick despatch to the colonies. Surtees was far from hopeless but there was no military or episcopal tradition in the family and so he was sent to the law.

Even so it is surprising that his father chose for him the minor and much less socially acceptable branch of the profession and articled him to a solicitor. One would have thought it far more likely that the squire of Hamsterley would have sent his son to the Bar. Perhaps the explanation is that all his hopes were centred on Anthony the elder son and, after the fashion of the day, cared little what happened to his brother so long as he was given a profession of a sort and the means of supporting himself. Another and more likely explanation is that with a large family to rear and the expense of two packs of hounds, funds simply did not run to keeping the younger brother during the long period in the early life of a barrister when briefs would be slow in coming. The possibility of permanent failure in the hazardous profession of advocacy may have played a part, too.

Robert left Durham School in 1819 and, according to the Law Society records, was not articled as a solicitor until 1822, three years later when he was seventeen. It has been suggested that, during these years, he was working as a clerk in the office of the solicitor to whom he was later articled, and this is as good an explanation as we are likely to get. Certainly wherever he received it and however reluctantly he acquired it he had a good grounding in the law and a comprehensive knowledge of it both in theory and practice. From 1822 for the next three years the account is clear: he was articled to Mr Robert Anthony Purvis, solicitor, of Newcastle, with a view to becoming a solicitor himself and practising law, and he hated every minute of it.

At the end of the third year something happened to

determine the association, no one knows just what. It may have been that Surtees, detesting the law as we know he did, and being all his life a quarrelsome man, simply fell out with his master. Whatever the reason a decision was made to send him to London to continue his articles. Surtees himself gives no hint of the cause of his removal from Newcastle, noting only that 'in the genial spring of 1825 I went to London'. He made the journey by coach:

I travelled up from Newcastle-on-Tyne by the old Highflyer coach, to catch which at eight o'clock in the morning I had to leave Hamsterley between five and six. Then, by a steady persevering grind continued all that day, all that night, and all the following day, we reached the dismal White Horse in Fetter Lane at eight that night. The fare was £6 inside and it was considered very fine travelling.

From Newcastle to York the journey was along the road lying over the high hilltops, and the vehicle was often drawn by very inferior horses. But after York where the passengers dined, there was visible improvement.... Luckless indeed was the passenger who had to stay at the White Horse but the coaching inns were all alike in those days... their inside accommodation and provision were about as uncomfortable as could be. Anything was thought good enough for a stagecoach passenger.[4]

In London he was 'further articled' to Mr William Bell of Bow Churchyard on his twentieth birthday. He was tall and spare, standing six feet one inch, and throughout his life he never lost the slim figure of his youth. His features, too, were already set in a serious mould. He rarely smiled and even at that early age appeared to be looking on the world with a lawyer's cool detachment. He was poor, for his father could manage no generous allowance such as sons of the wealthier aristocrats and magnates were given; he was unknown and friendless, for he had been furnished with no introductions. He had to make his own way and his own friends. All his life he was a reserved, solitary man; these traits and his temperament made things more difficult for him. He was lonely as only a young man alone in a great city can be lonely, and he was homesick and unhappy. Boodle's Club in St James's Street was the haunt and rendezvous of the country-breds, squires, and Masters of Foxhounds when they came to town, but Surtees had no entrée into clubland. The milieu in which he had to mix lay elsewhere and though he hated it he learnt much of the seedier, seamier side of the London of the day because of it, and he drew on his experiences in his writings later on.

In his book *Handley Cross* Surtees has left a record of the entry of Charley Stobbs, a young law student from the north of England, into chambers and London life and his reactions to them both. Since Surtees as a writer was a recorder and a remembrancer who drew almost entirely on observation and recollection rather than imagination, we can be sure that Charley Stobbs in this instance is himself and Charley's reactions Surtees's own:

Charley Stobbs was the only son of a rich Yorkshire yeoman, a man who, clinging to the style of his ancestors, called himself gentleman instead of esquire—gentlemen they had been styled for many generations and son had succeeded sire without wishing for a change. The old-latticed windowed manor house, substantial and stone-roofed, stood amid lofty oaks upon a gentle eminence above the level of a rapid river—myriads of rooks nestled in the branches and the rich meadows around were studded with gigantic oaks and weather-beaten firs.

Handley Cross, Chapter 24

It sounds exactly like Hamsterley recollected in the thoughts of an unhappy, homesick youth.

Charley Stobbs is not made welcome in chambers, for the Honourable Henry Lollington, one of the first of Surtees's drawling, vapid aristocrats whom he loathed all his life and upon whom he poured forth so much venom, immediately dubs him 'a snob' and the other members, taking their tone from their leader, ignore the newcomer. He is, however, befriended by Mr Bowker the clerk, who introduces him to no less a person than Mr Jorrocks and together they explore the steamy sporting underworld of London. On their first meeting they visit a 'hell' off High Holborn where bulldog matches and fighting, bear and badger-baiting, all unsparingly described, take place. 'That introduction', Surtees goes on to say, 'ripened into intimacy and many were the excursions our friends had together, Jorrocks finding cash and the Yorkshireman company.' This is almost certainly autobiographical though the identity of the friend who took him up, out on expeditions, and who found the cash, remains a mystery. It may well have been the man upon whom Jorrocks was based and of whom we know nothing, for Surtees has left only a few fragmentary and contradictory clues as to his identity. At all events he appears to have saved Surtees/Stobbs from despair, and from ending his career, for Surtees goes on to say: 'But for Jorrocks and perhaps Belinda [Jorrocks's niece] Stobbs would very soon have left the law whose crotchety quibbles are enough to digust anyone with a taste for truth and straightforward riding.'

The law, as practised then and as Surtees saw it, was a tough, hard profession not free from chicanery. His portraits of lawyers are, with one exception, scathing in the extreme. Charley Stobbs's very first master was 'one of those legal nuisances called conveyancers, whom it is hoped that some legal loophole will be found to extinguish, and he could find a loophole for an unwilling purchaser to creep out at in the very best of titles'. And of the attorney in *Ask Mamma* he is even more censorious:

Mr Carroty Kebbell was a huge red-haired, Crimean-bearded peripatetic attorney, who travelled from petty sessions to petty sessions spending his intermediate time at public houses, ferreting out and getting-up cases. He was a roistering ruffian who contradicted everybody, denied everything and tried to get rid of what he couldn't answer with a horse-laugh. He was in good practice for he allowed the police a liberal percentage on bringing him prosecutions, while his bellowing, bullying insured him plenty of defences on his own account.

Chapter 90

Surtees's loathing of the legal profession was shared by several of his literary contemporaries or near contemporaries: Sir Walter Scott, Dickens, Thackeray, Harrison Ainsworth, Charles Reade, and R. D. Blackmore all dabbled in law as a profession and left it either in dudgeon or disgust. All Surtees's talents and ambitions lay far from legal chambers. His heart was with horses and hounds and not with the dusty and, he believed, in many cases dirty and dishonest tergiversations of the law. His science was that of venery and not of jurisprudence. And all the time he had within him, crying to get out, the urge to write, that *cacoethes scribendi* which he called 'a taste for scribbling' from which, once it is born in a man, he can never rid himself.

But he did qualify. In 1828 he was 'admitted to Chancery' and set up his plate at 27 Lincoln's Inn Fields where he occupied the bachelor living quarters above the chambers. A year earlier Charles Dickens had been employed for the first time in a solicitor's office in Gray's Inn. Their paths were never to cross.

Whatever Surtees did he did with immense application and a whole heart. Thus, though he hated the law he mastered it, and something of his legal training and practice stayed with him throughout his life for his books are studded with legal terms, characters, and phraseology. He described lawyers as a whole as 'able, un'able and lamentable'. It is probable that he himself fell into the first class for although once he was qualified his thoughts turned elsewhere and his sporting and writing activities took him away from his office for longer and longer periods, he appears to have succeeded in supporting himself by his legal activities for some years before he became established in journalism.

CHAPTER TWO

Brighton and Boulogne

THE year 1829 was an important one for Surtees—he discovered Brighton and he began to write. His thoughts were now turning entirely away from the law towards sport and journalism but since he had no private means he still had to earn a living. Somehow, probably by keeping long hours and giving every attention to clients on the days he did work, he managed it. It has to be remembered, too, that courts sat less frequently, and the demands on professional men were far less pressing then than now. At all events, as he says himself, 'the winter of 1829 brought me to Brighton'. There he hunted with the Brookside Harriers, the Brighton Harriers, and the East Sussex Foxhounds, subsequently the Southdown, and enjoyed himself immensely. To reach Brighton he again travelled by coach for 'the best covert hacks in the world' as Mr Jorrocks dubbed the railways, had not yet reached the south coast.

Coaching, during those few years before the spread of the railway antennae, had reached its apogee, and competition between the various lines was intense. Not only that but the fashion set during the Regency by Sir John Lade and his wife, Letty, for aristocrats and gentlemen to be on the various boxes, 'tooling the ribbons' was still flourishing. The two leaders amongst these were Henry Stevenson and Sir St Vincent Cotton, both Etonians and Cambridge men who piloted The Age, Surtees's favourite coach, on the Brighton run.

For comfort, punctuality, and general smartness The Age was unrivalled on the Brighton road. The coach itself was painted black, picked out in red, and bore only its name 'The Age' and destination: 'From London to Brighton' or vice versa, on its bodywork. The horses were the best that money could buy, the fare was twelve shillings outside or one pound inside. The whole affair was known, Surtees tells us, as 'The Lion of the Road'; there was always a crowd to see the entourage start and at selected stages a silver box containing sandwiches together with a flask of sherry were passed around amongst the passengers. By using The Age Surtees made sure that his experiences on the Durham run when he first came to London would not be repeated.

Once arrived in Brighton the traveller had his pick of the smart hotels—the York, the Albion, the Ship, and the Gloucester. 'The sea dashed against the windows of the Albion, for there was then no roadway in front, and the Pool valley, like the isthmus of Suez, was the only link between the two ends of the town.'

Just why Surtees chose Brighton as a base for his sporting expeditions is a mystery since, as he himself tells us, Brighton at that time was a cliqueish and exclusive town, its society composed of a number of 'sets' and, if you did not belong to one of them, you remained an outsider. Surtees was not 'on a lady patroness's list' and had none of the required introductions. He became therefore, as he so often was, a detached observer, watching the antics of others with a cynical and appraising eye. One of the first to catch his attention and to be pinned like a butterfly to the specimen board of his recollection was the Brighton 'Master of Ceremonies' Captain Eld. The description of him that he wrote long afterwards is an epitome of Surtees's satiric method with an appropriate sting in the tail:

Captain Eld long held the honourable office of *Arbiter Elegantiarum*, as the newspapers used to designate the office; and his chief duty seemed to be watching the various coaches as they entered Brighton, running the newcomers to ground at their hotels or lodgings, digging them out, as it were, with a highly-glazed card, which bore the talismanical name 'Captain Eld, M.C.' printed on it. There were two public . . . libraries and at each . . . lay a large red-backed book devoted to the receipt of subscriptions to the captain's emoluments. In these books the recipients of the aforesaid cards were expected to

11

enter their names and addresses, with the much more interesting addition of One, one, opposite. They were then entitled to get what they could for their guinea, which might be briefly described by the little word *Nil*.[1]

Captain Eld was duly immortalized in print later on as Captain Miserrimus Doleful, Master of Ceremonies, self-appointed, in that rising spa Handley Cross.

Because he was a sensitive, touchy man Surtees may well have felt the social indignity of being overlooked. However, it was not for society that he came to Brighton, it was for sport, and here he was entirely at home. 'I know of nothing more beautiful than a run on those springy downs on a fine, sunny day', he wrote long afterwards when he had seen more of hounds and hunting in many different countries than most men. It was indeed the sort of hunting best suited to his tastes and talents, bearing a resemblance to that of the rough country in which he had been brought up and to which he remained devoted all his life.

Surtees was never either an accomplished or a bold horseman. He was a hound man, and to him the skill of the huntsman together with the ability of his hounds to pursue and track down their quarry was everything. The fences were not obstacles to be surmounted with bravado and dash but unpleasant impediments to the true exploitation of the huntsman's art. Like many such men and Masters of Hounds right down to the present day he had a disinclination for leaving the ground. 'A fall is a h'awful thing' says Jorrocks J. and the sentiment comes straight from the heart of his creator. Besides, a fall interrupted the real business of the chase—that of watching your hounds work and helping them where necessary.

'It's the dash of the 'ound, the feathering for the scent, the picking it out, the challenge when it's found, the rush of the pack to the cry—the werry sight of the beauteous, mottled intelligent h'animals is enough to set my werry blood boiling.'

Handley Cross, Chapter 33

This was the creed and justification of the fox-hunter, and an attitude that contributed to the clash of personalities with Nimrod some years later.

There was in any event little likelihood of falls when hunting from Brighton for there were few obstacles on the open downs, though there were other difficulties to be surmounted which only added to the interest:

The mists or fogs sometimes hang densely about the hills after leaving the low grounds, enveloping the sportsmen in unexpected clouds. They may ride and ride to the music of hounds without seeing them. I remember a run of this sort with Colonel Wyndham from Applesham gorse over the downs in the season of which I am speaking (1829), as hard as hounds could go, in which nobody ever saw anything save indistinct mythical-looking horsemen flying through the fog, until the hounds killed their fox down in the clear atmosphere of the valley below.[2]

And there was plenty of time, too, for observing the characters who made up the field. Surtees always had an eye for the absurd, and amongst those who hunted from Brighton that season was a certain Baron Gablenz:

The Baron, who was quite a young man not more than two or three-and-twenty, I should think . . . had a couple of valets, an Englishman and a Frenchman—one to dress his person, the other to dress his hair. The former, whose name was White, or Vite, as the Baron pronounced it . . . was not a great hand at turning a gentleman out for the chase. . . . One day he appeared in an uncommonly gay-coloured cut velvet evening vest with steel buttons that had been doing duty overnight at Almacks or elsewhere. On my telling him that he would be sure to spoil his fine vest, he exclaimed, 'Oh, by my word, Sortee, there is nothing too good for foxin' in!'[3]

The Baron appears in print in *Hawbuck Grange* and, in more detail, as Prince Pirouetteza in *Plain or Ringlets?* written thirty years after Surtees had seen him, and almost exactly as he had described him then.

During the summer of 1829 Surtees ventured abroad for the first time, spending his holidays first in Paris and then at Boulogne. Of his stay in Paris nothing is known but at

Boulogne he found plenty to interest and amuse him in the way of hounds and hunting, sport and sporting or semi-sporting characters. It was the beginning of August when he arrived there but hounds, such as they were, were already out. Boulogne just then shared with Calais the dubious distinction of being the resting place for English 'swells' who had made their own country too hot to hold them because of an inability to settle with their creditors or for other good reasons. 'Many things', Surtees was later to write, 'contribute to thin the ranks of our swells. Many...outrun the constable. Some get fat, some get married, some get tired, and a few get wiser.'[4] None of those then resident at Boulogne had got wiser; most of them had outrun the constable, and the fact that they had bolted from their English creditors did not prevent them running up accounts with French tradesmen which they declined, or were unable, to pay. The French authorities had no hesitation in imprisoning for debt with the result that many of these expatriates were housed in the local gaol which the towns-people promptly christened the 'Hôtel d'Angleterre'.

Swells, half-swells or broken-down swells were types Surtees detested and it is no wonder that, surveying the motley crew by which he was surrounded, he should comment, 'the gay town of Boulogne [was] one of the pleasantest if not the most respectably inhabited, in France. Since whatever may have been its deficiencies in the latter respect, however, were attributed to the English, so perhaps the less said on that score the better.'[5] His distaste for the company in which he found himself did not prevent him from observing them and making his usual acid comments on their habits and eccentricities.

The leader of society (if it could be called that) in Boulogne was Brooke Richmond, 'being to it what Brummel was to Calais'. Richmond was said once, for a bet, to have ridden down St James's Street mounted on a cow to the great shock and astonishment of those in society, and of the *haut ton* who were gathering for entry to the Palace. He was accompanied everywhere by a white bulldog which he pampered outrageously and which once turned on his master, taking him by the throat in a post-chaise because he had not been provided with a proper bed to sleep upon on the journey. Or so Richmond said, boasting all the time, 'Depend upon it he is a proper dog', while continuing to cosset him after this adventure. Richard Martin, MP for Galway, 'Humanity Dick' who had sponsored the bill for prevention of cruelty to animals, was there, too, and for the same reason as the majority—an inability to settle his debts. Hunting, Surtees comments, was not classified by him as a cruel sport for he used to ride out every day to meet the hounds and enquire how they had done and what sport they had had. And there were others who fell victim to Surtees's probing eye and sharp comment but soon he found a reason which above all others persuaded him to prolong his stay at Boulogne.

One day while out hacking he heard the cry of hounds. In a minute or two a hare crossed the road in front of him followed, after an appreciable interval, by a pack of hounds. They were being hunted by, or rather accompanied by, a 'portly elderly gentleman dressed in a lowish-crowned hat with a green frock coat and top-boots mounted on a good-looking bay horse. His servant, similarly attired, was also well mounted.' Surtees, it may be mentioned in passing, was a meticulous dresser himself, 'something of a dandy', one who remembered him well recorded. He always had an eye for the clothes worn by others be they male or female and in his books he describes them in almost wearisome detail, down to the last button and spur-strap.

Telling the huntsman that the hare had crossed, Surtees watched him as he made a leisurely cast forward. Scent was, however, very catchy and although the hounds recovered the line they could do little with it and after a few fields the chase was abandoned. Riding home together Surtees found that his companion was a Mr Sackville Cresswell, 'a gentleman accustomed to his comforts of which a pack of hounds was one'. A racecourse was another and he had established one among the sand-dunes near his villa at Hardelot some miles from Boulogne. Unfortunately, as with most of the 'swells', Mr

Cresswell's means failed to keep pace with this magnificence. They expired altogether very soon after he and Surtees met with the result that Mr Cresswell was duly taken off and incarcerated in the Hôtel d'Angleterre.

A pack of hounds, as Surtees remarks, is just about as much use to a man in gaol as a riding-master to the Doge of Venice and so Mr Cresswell asked his new friend if he would take on the hounds together with a Colonel Charrittie, another sporting worthy recently arrived to take up temporary residence in Boulogne.

Colonel Charrittie, an Irishman who as a very young man had served with the Life Guards at Waterloo, had a 'taste for dissipation and high play' which may have caused his removal to Boulogne, but there could also have been other reasons. A flamboyant character who had fought several duels and emerged unscathed from each, Charrittie was no respecter of persons nor of other people's property, and when shooting was an inveterate poacher. Once when the Marquis of Salisbury was inspecting his coverts with his head keeper the keeper had occasion to point out Charrittie to him, saying: 'There he is on your Lordship's land again'. Salisbury, who was riding a cob which was a special favourite of his, dismounted. Giving the cob to the keeper he told him to ride on and shoot Charrittie's dog. 'That will stop him and teach him a lesson,' he said. The keeper mounted the cob, went ahead and obeyed his instructions, killing the dog, whereupon Charrittie raised his own gun, shot the cob, and told the terrified man he was lucky not to have suffered the same fate.

The Marquis, infuriated, at first demanded satisfaction, sending no less a person than Squire Osbaldeston as his emissary to carry the challenge. Osbaldeston, the 'Squire of England' as he was called, was probably at that time the most formidable man in the country. Certainly he was one of the best pistol shots, and was reputed to shoot the pip out of the ace of diamonds at thirty paces just to keep his hand in. He was, besides, a sportsman supreme, Master of Foxhounds, cross-country rider, cricketer, and marathon walker. Whether these two, Charrittie and Osbaldeston, recognized in each other a kindred spirit it is impossible to say, but certainly the matter was settled. The Marquis, perhaps reminded by Osbaldeston of Charrittie's prowess with a pistol, withdrew his challenge and had recourse to the more formal remedies of the law. This may or may not have been the incident—for there were many more like it—which compelled Charrittie to leave England and seek sanctuary in Boulogne.

At all events these two unlikely characters, Surtees and Charrittie, came together to take over Mr Cresswell's hounds. It was perhaps fortunate that the association was not a long one since both were high-tempered men always ready for a fight; a final falling-out was inevitable and Charrittie's readiness with the duelling pistol combined with Surtees's pugnacity and stubbornness might have resulted in disaster. It is also perhaps fortunate that Charrittie, by then a General (though most of his subsequent career had been concerned with organizing the new sport of steeplechasing and arranging matches, usually to his own profit) did not recognize himself, hideously traduced, in the portrait of Johnny O'Dicey, the shady clubman-gambler who appeared in *Plain or Ringlets?* nearly thirty years later.

However, at the time all went well. The first problem was to find out the names of the hounds since the only hunt servant had decamped on hearing the news of his master's arrest. This was overcome with the assistance of the gaoler who brought one of the Masters to the upstairs room in the Hôtel d'Angleterre where Mr Cresswell was comfortably housed, while the other paraded hounds below the window in batches of five, Mr Cresswell naming them as they passed.

The next difficulty was finding something to hunt. Hares were scarce, and most of those that were about were shot by the locals who in any event resented the hunt trampling their gardens and smallholdings, smashing their fences and generally rampaging over the countryside. Summonses for trespass began to proliferate and so they turned their thoughts to fox. Foxes were plentiful amongst the dunes around Mr Cresswell's empty villa but they would not run and the riding, of course, was atrocious over such sandy and treacherous ground.

It was then that one of them, almost certainly Charrittie, thought of a solution. A Mr George Templer bred, owned, and hunted a pack of dwarf foxhounds in the West Country. He would not allow them to taste blood and had brought them to such a state of discipline that they would not kill. However, in order to provide a quarry he collected wild foxes which he kept in captivity, drawing a certain number each day which he unleashed before his hounds. Amazingly enough he showed very good sport. The joint masters put their problem before Mr Templer who agreed to come over and supervise the capture and training of foxes to run before the Boulogne Hounds. Very soon they had a sufficient number in the care of an Englishman who kept an inn some miles outside the town, and they were impatient to get started. Because they were not quite sure of the stoutness of the first fox they were to enlarge they decided to run a partial drag, turning down the bagman when the drag ran out. (Both Mr Jorrocks and Mr Facey Romford used exactly the same technique with a bagman with great success during their fictional fox-hunting adventures.) The ruse worked, the fox ran far straighter and faster than ever expected and a rattling hunt ensued. 'Never saw such a run!' 'Finest fox that ever was seen!', Surtees recorded as some of the exclamations of his gratified field.

Thenceforward sport improved vastly, more and more people began to come out and more and more often the hunt left the sand-hills for the open country. But unfortunately, once more, the landowners' wrath was incurred. Matters came to a head when they ran their fox into an old gentleman's cottage. Five francs having been paid to keep him quiet Mr Templer proceeded to search the cottage and found the tip of the fox's brush just showing under the counterpane on the owner's bed. The five francs did not, however, prove sufficient to silence the old gentleman. He complained to the local press who blew the whole thing up into a resounding scandal as a consequence of which armed gendarmes were deputed to ride with the hunt to prevent landowners and peasantry from further insult and outrage. The gendarmes, however, could not keep up and the *gardes-champêtre* were much more difficult to deal with. 'These came upon the parties unaware, popping out from behind stone walls and any sort of ambuscade that would cover them, and cutting the horse's bridle reins before he was aware of their presence.'[6]

All this sounds far more as if it were inspired by Charrittie than Surtees who, even at the age of twenty-four, was a law-abiding young man. The whole thing ended, as might have been expected, especially in any enterprise where Charrittie was concerned, in uproar and blazing farce.

Once the activities of the authorities had made hunting, at least in the immediate environs of Boulogne, too uncomfort-able, the joint masters took themselves and their hounds to a village called Samer about ten miles away. Samer existed on the manufacture of gloves made from the skins of foxes and hares caught and killed in the locality and it was thought that they might welcome the assistance of two 'Lords Rosbif' to kill more of their raw material for them.

To make sure that they would not suffer any interference Surtees and Charrittie arranged for a joint meet with the local pack who hunted the foxes and hares for their skins, and to provide extra goodwill for their gallop they gave a great dinner for the local worthies.

The dinner, at least, was a success; Monsieur Saurange, the postmaster and one of the chief dignitaries present was carried home at midnight on a shutter.

On the day of the joint meet a sort of hilarious madness took control of the proceedings. 'The French marched off to the *chasse* in military array with guns and carbines, playing on numerous twisted horns. . . . Soon "Bang! Bang!" went a couple of guns as if a keeper were out after the cock, though in reality it was a Frenchman letting drive at the fox.' The joint masters had generously presented two useless hounds, Warrior and Wonderful, to their hosts. 'One was an incorrigible babbler and skirter, the other would only do what he liked which was generally nothing.' These however, on this day, hunted everything and the French hounds, 'old knock-kneed animals' hunted them. 'Their sonorous notes roused the denizens of the woods, and then the scattered sportsmen intercepted these and knocked them over as best they could. That was what they called a *chasse,* and when they had exterminated the hare we saw Warrior and Wonderful in pursuit of some other quarry.'[7]

On returning to Boulogne they found that their earlier trespasses and misdeeds had borne fruit in the shape of sheaves of summonses for every conceivable offence and misdemeanour affecting other people's property. Hastily the joint masters took ship for England. Surtees landed at Dover just in time for the opening day of the season with Mr Oxenden's Hounds in East Kent. They were rather different from those with which he had recently been associated, 'an uncommonly pretty lot, in beautiful condition and well turned out'.

He was looking forward to a good season's hunting but it was not to be. Very soon the weather closed in; it was to be the hardest winter in recent years, hounds were stopped entirely for two months, and even before and after the worst of the frost could only go out intermittently. Having little else with which to occupy his spare time Surtees decided to indulge his 'taste for scribbling'. First he made an attempt at what he described as 'a semi-sporting novel'. When he had written two-thirds of it he showed it to two friends who, having read it, derided it. If it was in the same vein as his later work, as one can safely assume it must have been, this is not surprising for Surtees was all his life outside the mainstream of the fiction of the day. He was, as we shall see, a throwback to an earlier, lustier age which was one of the reasons success was so slow in coming to him. The general public who fed on romance, gallants, great-hearts, and women who swooned at a touch or a kiss could not understand why he concerned himself with characters mostly sprung from the underworld of sport who could be, and immediately were branded as undesirable in the prevailing social and moral climate. Apart from that the book was obviously a prentice work, his first attempt, and most novelists are well advised to destroy their initial immature offerings. Surtees did just that. He put it in the fire.

But the urge to write would not leave him. He began to turn his knowledge of the law and horse-dealing to account and to jot down notes for what was to be, in 1831, his first published book: *The Horseman's Manual; being a treatise on Soundness, the law of Warranty, and generally on the laws relating to Horses.* More importantly, however, having been discouraged by the reception of his novel he remembered that he had been held to write a good essay at school, and he determined to try his hand at journalism. He turned out some hunting sketches and sent them to the editor of the *Sporting Magazine.*

If later on he was to be unfortunate because his books were so far removed from the literary fashion and taste of the day, he was singularly lucky in the moment he chose to submit those hunting articles. For the proprietors of the *Sporting Magazine* had just fallen out with the man who had made its fortune, the famous Nimrod, the first and greatest hunting correspondent of all time.

CHAPTER THREE

Nimrod

CHARLES JAMES APPERLEY, 'Nimrod' to the sporting press and public, was everything Surtees was not, and embodied in himself, his career, and his writings most things Surtees scorned and detested. When Surtees arrived in London in 1825 poor, young, and unknown, Nimrod was at the very height of his fame. Surtees read his articles. From that moment on, although he had no personal acquaintance with their author and was not to have for some years, he appears to have conceived a virulent antipathy towards him, an antipathy which, however, he could and did conceal when occasion suited him.

Nimrod was born in 1778 into a Denbighshire County family, the son of a man who was both a sportsman and a scholar, and he was educated at a great public school, Rugby, where he acquired a taste for the classics. During the holidays at Plasgronow, the family home, he enjoyed field sports as Surtees did at Hamsterley, and soon proved himself an efficient and dashing horseman and rider to hounds.

After Rugby an attempt was made to apprentice him to one of the great Guilds but, just as Surtees loathed the law he hated and despised commerce, and finally he was commissioned into Sir Watkin Wynne's fencible cavalry, the Ancient British Light Dragoons, with whom he saw service during the Irish Rebellion of 1898. During the insurrection the regiment earned for itself the sobriquet 'Bloody Britons' and it was notorious for the savage cruelties it inflicted on the inhabitants and for the heavy drinking amongst its officers. After the suppression of the rebellion the regiment remained on at The Curragh where Nimrod commenced his racing career with a mare which won six races for him at one meeting. He was an excellent judge of a horse and whilst serving in Ireland he commenced a career in horse-dealing which he was to pursue with success for much of his life. The heavy drinking of his fellow officers had its influence on him with the result that he narrowly escaped becoming an alcoholic and, having done so, he remained a most moderate drinker ever afterwards. When the regiment was disbanded he took up coaching and became almost as proficient with the ribbons as Stevenson and Sir St Vincent Cotton were later to become.

At this period of his life Nimrod was drifting, as he was to be for much of his subsequent career. He was an extraordinarily handsome young man, gay, attractive, and presentable, with a winning manner and address. A beautiful horseman with exquisite hands he could cross any country that confronted him, mounted on almost anything, in the very first flight. Although he was all but penniless, having soon exhausted the fund his father had settled on him early in life, it was no surprise to anyone when he made a good match. He married a Miss Elizabeth Wynne, a distant cousin of his own and a kinswoman of Sir Watkin's. The Wynnes were rich and quite happy, apparently, to support the young pair, indeed his father-in-law never lost the affection he felt for him and kept contributing to his support on and off through every vicissitude of his eventful life.

The couple were soon established at Hinkley in Leicestershire. Mr Meynell, whom all his life Nimrod admired in much the same way as did Surtees Ralph Lambton, had just given up the Quorn Hounds but his successor, Lord Sefton, did things in even greater style. Nimrod was instantly fascinated by the glamour and the panache, the pace, the dash, the swagger, and the go with which the whole thing was carried on. He had found what was to be forever afterwards his favourite pack and his spiritual home amongst 'the cream of the cream in the shire of the shires'.

The individuals who made up the fields of the shire packs, especially that of the Quorn and those based on Melton

Mowbray, the fashionable centre ('Meltonians' as they were called), operated at that time and indeed to some extent have since, what was in the nature of a social closed shop. They were smart, worldly, and rich. Mounted on the best that money could buy, the galloping grass acres over which their hounds ran provided the fastest and best hunting in England. They were exclusive and intended to remain so, scorning the slower, rougher, provincial packs, many of which nevertheless had deeper roots in rural England, as Surtees later took pains in his writing to point out. Visitors from outside or from the provinces were dubbed 'snobs' by the Meltonians; they were cold-shouldered at the meet and ran the risk of being ridden over in the field. The word 'snob' itself had a different connotation in those days. Surtees later scornfully described the Meltonian definition as 'an unfortunate stranger in a country-cut coat in the hunting field'. The Meltonians themselves, however, preferred that found in the dictionary: 'a vulgar and ostentatious person, one who has no pretensions to rank or gentility'.

Qualifications for admission to the charmed circle of true Meltonians were good breeding and good connections, combined with the ability to ride at least as well as themselves (they would never admit that anyone could do it better) and 'to send your heart over in front and then follow it in the best way you can' when faced by any obstacle however fearsome.

Nimrod started with three great advantages. He was bred well enough to pass muster and had married well; he had good looks and charming manners, two things your true Meltonian admired more than most, and he took care to see that he was superbly mounted. Then, too, and this above all franked his passport to success, when hounds were running he crossed the country as if he had fire in his blood. One who watched him ride to hounds with a strange pack a little later said of him: 'When I saw him first with Lord Derby's Hounds he was a stranger to everyone, but he soon attracted notice. At the second check it was asked who it was on the chestnut?'[1]

Thus he gained immediate acceptance into the hearts and favours and inner circle of Meltonians, and he revelled in it.

All his life Nimrod loved the company of the great, the fashionable, and the smart but above and beyond that he was fascinated by the quality of the sport shown. Pace meant everything to him—pace, excitement, drama, the thrill of a blood horse jumping big beneath him. Then, too, there was the competition, the pleasure of 'cutting-down' the other swells or trying to, and of riding each hunt as if it were a race. Not for him the huntsman's skills in worrying out the way a fox had gone on a bad scenting day in a rough country. He never did, in fact, master the intricacies in the huntsman's art, which earned him Surtees's scorn. It was enough for Nimrod that hounds were running and running on straight as a gun-barrel from Ashby Pastures or Barkby Holt. No wonder he and Surtees, who were to become the leading writers of their day on fox-hunting, found themselves diametrically opposed in their attitudes to the sport.

Nimrod's conception of fox-hunting was utterly alien to that of Surtees. Moreover, at a time when Nimrod was sailing across High Leicestershire in the company of the swells and writing effusively about it and them, Surtees could only afford a few stolen days with suburban packs. As he made Mr Jorrocks say in a passage surely written out of recollection and from the heart:

'London's a grand place, to be sure . . . but oh, my beloved 'earers, there is no misery like that of solitude in a crowd, or inconwenience like that of livin' with men without being able to afford to partake o' their plissurs. London's the rich man's paradise, the poor man's puggatory!'

Handley Cross, Chapter 59

Given those feelings about his existence in the city and his natural temperament, it is not surprising that he felt envious of Nimrod and his success.

Nimrod's residence at Hinkley lasted three years and the family then moved to Bilton Hall in Worcestershire where Nimrod stabled his horses in three different counties so that he could be within hacking distance (sometimes, however, twenty miles or more) of the best meets in each. He took good care, too, to get back to the Shires whenever he could, his favourite, as always, being the Quorn.

Unfortunately for him, as was to happen throughout his life, his tastes far outran his means. He was mixing with some of the wealthiest man in the kingdom and was determined that in every way, horseflesh ('a man with five hunters and a hack', he recorded, 'makes a very respectable appearance in the provinces, but he has no business in Leicestershire'),[2] saddlery, turn-out, hacks, and servants, he should not be outdone by any of them.

It could not last and the end of that period of his life came fairly quickly. He moved to Carnarvonshire where his wife's family found him some sort of part-time employment as an estate agent. He took good care, however, that the employment did not interfere with his sporting pursuits. He went shooting in due season and to augment his income continued his horse-dealing activities. In order to further these he set up a small racing stable which he ran with considerable success, riding many of his horses as a 'gentleman jockey' himself. And, of course, he hunted, stealing away on visits to his beloved grass countries whenever he could. It was during this time that he made the acquaintance of 'Mad Jack' Mytton of Halston whose life he was later to write. Mytton was an eccentric and dissolute Shropshire squire whose antics included setting his night-shirt on fire to cure his hiccups. A bold and brilliant horseman, a fine shot and, when sober, a charming companion, Mytton's taste for drink and dissipation eventually ruined a splendid constitution, squandered a fine fortune and, in the end, killed him.

Nimrod was often at Halston and it is evidence of his kindly nature that he did what he could to restrain his friend's excesses. 'If all people who frequented Halston had been like Captain Apperley', one of the old servants said after Mytton's squalid death in delirium in the King's Bench Prison, 'Mr Mytton would never have come to any harm.' He remained Mytton's friend, too, after all the money had gone, providing at his own expense board and lodging for him in France where Mytton had gone to avoid his creditors.

Halston was not the only house he visited. In addition to his travels to the Shires he was hunting with neighbouring packs which often entailed putting up himself and his horses far from home. Such was his charm of manner and general agreeableness that long before his fame as a hunting correspondent had opened all doors to him, both he and his horses were welcome guests in great houses everywhere he went.

Then ill fortune struck again. There was a rift in the family. No one knows what caused it nor did Nimrod ever enlarge upon it in his later autobiographical writings. But he was never a domestic animal and his all too frequent absences from home on sporting expeditions may have caused his wife to decide that little purpose would be served by attempting to continue to live under the same roof. Whatever the reason, in 1821 she removed herself and her children from the family home and took up residence at Hampton in Middlesex where she lived until her death thirteen years later.

When she moved Mrs Apperley took her patrimony with her. Without his wife's money and with his horse-dealing for once failing to prosper Nimrod was hard hit financially. He had to leave Brewood House, their Welsh Home, and take up lodgings at Blackfriars Road in London while his father-in-law entered into some complicated negotiations to see what could be done to provide for him. All this, being in the middle of the hunting season, was a sore torment to one of his tastes. He hated London and loathed city life and his spirits were for once cast down. But, although he could not know it, he was on the brink of such fame and success as he could not have conceived in his wildest dreams.

Rather as Surtees had done but for different reasons, he decided to write a book, 'upon hunting and other sports of which I have partaken'. Arranging an appointment with a Mr Henry Colburn of Conduit Street, a publisher of whom we shall hear again, he outlined his project. Colburn gave him qualified encouragement but asked for a specimen of his work and what we should now call a synopsis of the subject matter. Nimrod, who was nothing if not grandiloquent—it was one of his faults which was to be mercilessly pilloried by Surtees later on—replied. 'My style ... would be merely that of any educated person who had moved in good society; and for the matter, it would be the result of my experience in the sporting world.'[3]

As he left Colburn's office he met quite by chance an old hunting friend who advised him that he would be unwise to put all his fortunes, as it were, at risk in one book. Journalism, the friend said, offered a better chance of quicker returns and higher profits and he advised him to try the *Sporting Magazine.* Once again Nimrod's reply was quite in character: 'That will never do,' he said. 'It is a mere cockney concern. No gentleman writes for it.'

'Never mind that,' was the sensible reply. 'Take my advice and go to the proprietor of it. If you write for it other gentlemen and sportsmen will do so also.'

Nimrod did take his advice and arranged an appointment with Mr Pittman, the owner and editor. Mr Pittman was impressed with his knowledge and experience and engaged him forthwith as a hunting reporter and writer on sporting subjects. It was fashionable then and indeed has remained so for a sporting writer to adopt a pseudonym. The name chosen for the new writer was 'Nimrod', 'a mighty hunter before the Lord'. Events were to show how apt the name and description were.

Nimrod's first article appeared in the New Year's number of 1822. It was, as might have been expected, on 'Fox-hunting in Leicestershire'. Others followed and were immediately accepted and published. Despite the fact that, as he himself wrote, 'a whip has been much oftener in my right hand for the last twenty-five years than a pen', Nimrod's style was cultured yet at the same time vigorous and racy. The articles were informed, accurate, authoritative, and entertaining. Nothing like them had been seen before in sporting journalism. They were immediately and resoundingly successful. Very soon, when he made his hunting tours, on his appearance at a meet everyone from the Master downwards deferred to him. It became a sort of accolade to have one's name mentioned in his reports and members of the field vied with each other in catching his eye and attracting his attention. Each issue of the *Sporting Magazine* was snapped up instantly, and eagerly scanned.

On his hunting tours Nimrod was entertained at the great houses of the localities he visited. His opinion and advice were sought for on the qualities and conformation of horses and hounds and comparisons invited from him between the performances of both in the various countries in which he had hunted. He was also in demand as an official at race meetings, an interpreter of articles, and ultimate arbiter in sporting disputes. Nor was his fame and the success he brought to the magazine confined to the British Isles, for it spread both to the continent and the colonies. When the ship bearing mail and newspapers berthed at Calcutta, Colonel Nesbitt, Master of the Calcutta Hounds, went to meet her and to ask if there was any important news. 'There are three new Ministers in,' he was told. 'Hang the Ministry,' was the reply. 'Is Nimrod's Northern Tour out yet?'[4]

In two years Nimrod had more than doubled both the circulation of the magazine and its profit. Mr Pittman was not slow to show his appreciation. In 1824 he gave his famous correspondent what was for those days the princely salary of £1,500 a year, and the magazine undertook to be responsible for the upkeep of five hunters and a hack. Nimrod was also free to continue his horse-dealing activities as he liked and for which his peregrinations round the hunting countries gave him plenty of opportunity.

But Mr Pittman was astute enough to take steps to protect his investment. He insisted on Nimrod entering into a binding agreement not to write under that pseudonym for any other paper or magazine for a period of ten years. In addition there was the question of the insurance on his life which was considered essential for he was a hard rider in a hazardous profession. Nimrod effected such insurance in the sum of £2,000; the yearly premium of £93 10*s*. was paid by the magazine for the first year and deducted from his salary. In subsequent years, so Nimrod claimed, it would appear correctly, the premium was paid by the magazine and Mr Pittman assumed entire responsibility for it. Unfortunately, however, this agreement was not committed to paper which omission, together with the grant of the exclusive use of his name, was to cause Nimrod much trouble and grief a few years later.

In the meantime the sporting world was at his feet, and he revelled in his position. Surtees, however, accused him of being egotistical and vain, a toady and a tuft-hunter. 'Tuft-hunter' was one of Surtees's favourite expressions of abuse, meaning one who pays foolish and slavish obeisance to the great. Nimrod, Surtees said, 'dearly loved a lord' and would write nothing against one; he 'buttered up' the rich and the titled and ignored lesser persons and packs.

There is some truth in these accusations but Surtees, as usual when something or someone whom he really disliked caught hold of him, carried them too far. It is true that Nimrod was to some extent at least spoiled by adulation as, indeed, many successful authors are. It is true that Nimrod placed an exaggerated value on both his worth and his writings and, worse, sang his own praises, reciting compliments paid to him both in conversation and in his articles. His prose, too, at the height of his fame when he did not take care to control or prune it, at times became florid in the extreme and overloaded with classical quotations. Both of these failings gave Surtees the opportunity to guy and parody him.

It was, however, unfair of Surtees to imply and maintain that Nimrod was unwilling and unable to criticize the rich, the great, and the famous, and that he fawned on them for their patronage. Of one titled MFH he wrote that he required the example of others before riding up to his pack; and he once so criticized the turn-out of Osbaldeston's hounds as to induce that formidable man to lay pen to paper, an exercise he was not in the habit of carrying out, in a protest to the editor of the *Sporting Magazine*. This protest alleged that the criticism would not have been so pointed had he asked Nimrod to dinner. The reply he received was scathing in the extreme and contained a refusal to withdraw one word of what had been written. It took considerable courage, a quality that, whatever his detractors may have maintained, Nimrod never lacked, to enter into written or any other conflict with one so ready and accurate with his pistols as the 'Squire of England'.

It is certainly the case, however, that Nimrod did on occasion throw himself open to parody and to accusations of pretentiousness in pitching too high his uncritical adulation for everything to do with Melton and Meltonians. There was about hunting in the Shires then an all-pervading air of grandeur and splendour, and true-blue Meltonians exuded everywhere a too-conscious confidence in their own absolute superiority. In addition there can be no doubt that a certain element of the meretricious did enter into the whole affair making it, those such as Surtees held, foreign to the true sport and spirit of fox-hunting. On bad scenting days huntsmen frequently resorted to moving their hounds in front of them at a gallop from covert to covert and many of the field neither knew nor cared if there was a fox on foot so long as they were galloping and jumping. When there was a scarcity of foxes it was not unknown for this to be made good by purchase and importation from outside; and it was also true that some of the field went out for show and not for sport. There is something in the criticism written by Surtees after Nimrod's death:

There was always a disposition on the part of Nimrod to magnify Leicestershire and Leicestershire men with something beyond what they will fairly bear. No doubt it is a fine grass country and many famous sportsmen resort to it from all parts of the kingdom; but it also draws a lot of noisy, perfumed, chattering coxcombs, who have no idea of hunting and no real pleasure in the thing. . . . Neither do we subscribe to the doctrine that Leicestershire is the only country in the world that appears to have been intended for fox-hunting. Nay, we are Goth enough to know countries we prefer to it . . .

He quoted with derision the remark of a certain high-born, hard riding Meltonian: 'See what sport we might have if it weren't for these d—d hounds!', adding the savage comment, 'So much for attending to what they *profess* to go out for.'[5]

From the whole body of his writings both as journalist and author there is clear evidence that dislike of Nimrod and distaste of all that he stood for, a distaste amounting almost to disgust, became something of an obsession with Surtees. In his study of Surtees, Frederick Watson defines the relationship of the two men in these terms:

The dislike of Surtees for Nimrod was probably as much instinctive as deliberate. There is a natural inclination in taciturn, unpopular men to have a fling at those transparent creatures who, by their amiability and freedom from dark moods, move through life—or part of it—as though it were a continuous gala night.[6]

Nimrod always had people clamouring for his friendship and the privilege of knowing him better. One of these has left a memoir of him which is worth quoting to set against the 'Pomponius Ego' picture painted by Surtees which has passed—most unfairly—into posterity.

Nimrod was one of the most fascinating persons I ever saw, his figure perfect, light and active, his features handsome and eyes that sparkled with intelligence and humour; his countenance beaming with good-nature and gaiety. He was truly a *sunny* person; always prompt to oblige and promote the pleasure of his friends; full of harmless fun and humour; much readiness in conversation. One of his essential qualifications was, no doubt, this talent to amuse . . .[7]

At all events, whatever Surtees thought of him in the obscurity of his lawyer's office, the fashionable and sporting world was, just then, at Nimrod's feet. He moved to a mansion at Beaurepaire in Hampshire where he set himself up in the high style to which he considered his position in the world entitled him. He took several adjoining farms on lease but his farming activities, as may be imagined, were very much those of a gentleman who has other affairs to attend to. In his case those affairs were sporting ones. In winter he was, of course, away on his hunting tours; in summer his contract with Mr Pittman ensured that he had to cover other sporting events and his authoritative articles on racing, coursing, and coaching continued to keep the magazine in demand. He was a scrupulous journalist—even Surtees conceded his almost pedantic insistence on accuracy: 'He tied himself to facts,' Surtees wrote, 'and no general describing an engagement looked with greater scrutiny on his despatch than Nimrod did on his description of a run.'[8] His strict observance, too, of what we should now call a deadline, must have delighted his editor's heart: 'I have only twelve hours to write this and ride fifty-four miles for it must be in London tomorrow morning,' he wrote Pittman in a covering letter on one occasion, adding at the end, above his signature, 'Dated from the outside of my hack.'[9]

The farms did not prosper, and Nimrod was robbed by his bailiff. His expenses, too, were enormous, and this coupled with his disregard for anything but the very best made money slip through his fingers like quicksilver. His casual attitude to possessions out-lorded that of the lords he was said to love so dearly. 'I met Nimrod one day in St James's Street,' a friend recorded. 'He was looking very smart and well. As we were talking he dropped a clean glove in the kennel, so pulling off the other, he stamped them both underfoot.'[10]

In the six years he worked for Mr Pittman he drew £9,000 in salary and in addition received the expenses of his stud. His horse-dealing was also extremely profitable. In a note found amongst his papers he set down twenty-three horses he had bought for a total of 2,207 guineas and sold for 5,012 guineas, an average profit of 122 guineas on each transaction. This record by no means comprises the whole of his horse-dealing activities during those years. He bought shrewdly and sold well and was in high repute amongst those he dealt for, and he has also recorded that he never sold a horse as a good one without having proved him. Yet despite all this when the blow fell he had nothing left.

In 1827 Mr Pittman died. At first this made little difference to Nimrod and he carried on just as before. But when the executors of Mr Pittman's estate came to proceed with its administration they began to scrutinize in some detail the accounts of the magazine. They came to the conclusion, rightly or wrongly, that the princely salary and expenses paid to Nimrod were eating into its profits and were unjustified by the results. Surtees says that Mr Pittman before his death had himself become dissatisfied with the amounts paid to Nimrod and that the executors were only complying with his intentions in the step they next took.[11] Whether this is so or not it remains a fact that they entered into negotiations with Nimrod for a reduction of his salary and more especially of the expenses incurred in the upkeep of his stud. Instead of being responsible for the entire amount they offered him £170 a year as a contribution towards costs.

Nimrod would have none of this; he wanted more, not less. He considered, with some justification, that he had made the prosperity of the magazine, but he overreached himself when he declared himself to be indispensable and that without him the magazine would die. He delivered an ultimatum stating his terms and, fully confident that they would be accepted, departed on a hunting tour of Germany which he proposed to report for the magazine.

The tour, the last fanfare, as it were, of the great days of Nimrod, was a triumphant success. It ended in a blaze of glory when he was offered a ride in the Gold Cup at Dobberron on a difficult horse called Wildfire. Although he was then fifty years of age it was the sort of challenge he could not resist and he accepted. To do the weight he had to waste from 11st. 7lb. to 10st. 3lb. but it was all worth it for he won the race with a fair amount of ease.

At a dinner given in his honour that night, with a typically grandiloquent gesture he presented the cup together with his cap and jacket to the Grand Duchess of Mecklenburg, the patroness of the meeting and the dinner. She responded by having a replica of the cup made and given to him before he left the country.

Returning home, as he thought in triumph and with his reputation enhanced, he had no doubts that the executors would meet his demands. He was speedily disillusioned. In his absence the executors had given much thought to the matter. Whether they took legal and literary advice we do not know but we do know that Surtees later commented on the price Nimrod placed on himself and his writings: 'Nimrod had no notion of writing for nothing, and we question whether any man of such limited ability ever got such high prices as he did.'[12] It seems the executors took the same view. Nimrod's ultimatum was turned down.

Now Nimrod was confronted with the choice of continuing his employment on far worse terms than before or resigning. Still certain of the price he could command anywhere, he resigned.

There is no doubt that, blinded by his popularity and his successes and, overestimating his worth, he acted too hastily and without proper thought for the consequences. Immediately his resignation was in their hands the executors reminded him of his agreement with Mr Pittman not to use the name 'Nimrod' elsewhere than in his magazine for a period of ten years and that that period had not yet elapsed. Worse was to follow for in addition the executors had unearthed the transactions over the insurance premiums and they now demanded from Nimrod repayment of the amounts advanced by Mr Pittman on his behalf—as they claimed. They also stated that Mr Pittman had made other loans to him, and the total sum demanded amounted to £1,200. Nimrod had not the means to meet this sum which in any event he disputed, whereupon the executors issued a writ for its recovery.

Whatever the merits of the case (and there was certainly some independent evidence forthcoming from a member of the staff that Mr Pittman had accepted responsibility for the premiums), Nimrod had no financial resources at all and he could not afford to fight it. There was therefore nothing for it but to do as so many others did in similar circumstances and to seek safety abroad. He had to throw up his farms, abandon his home at Beaurepaire and sail for France in a hurry. All this, he said, led to a further loss of approximately £1,500. Perhaps he had been too high-handed, perhaps he had grown self-important, but in view of all he had done for the paper it is impossible not to accept that he was most shabbily treated.

This was certainly the view of his Meltonian friends who opened a subscription list for him. No less than 125 noblemen and gentlemen placed their names on the list and subscribed in all the sum of £1,327. Among the nobility the names included those of the Dukes of Buccleuch, Grafton, and Richmond, the Earls of Derby, Kintore, and Clonmell, and among the many distinguished Masters of Hounds were the signatures of Assheton Smith, Squire Osbaldeston, and Ralph Lambton. Nor did the members of the Old Club at Melton forget him for they came forward with a substantial contribution. It was a demonstration of how he had won his way into the hearts of those men whose bravery and dash across a country he could match with his own.

With this subscription and what little he could salvage from the sale of his effects Nimrod was able to set up house at the rue des Thermes in Calais at a rent of £42 a year. But his great days as a hunting and sporting correspondent were gone forever and on the *Sporting Magazine* Robert Smith Surtees stepped into his shoes.

CHAPTER FOUR

Journalist and Editor

SURTEES was not a success as a hunting correspondent. Partly this stemmed from the fact that, succeeding Nimrod, he was his exact antithesis. Where Nimrod's prose had been racy and highly coloured, Surtees's was pedestrian. Where Nimrod had been friendly and approachable, he was saturnine and aloof; where Nimrod 'buttered up', Surtees scoffed without mercy and in the plainest possible language. Two instances of his outspoken comment in the *Sporting Magazine* will suffice to show why he singularly failed to win his way, as Nimrod had done, into the affections of the hunts he visited. Here is his account of his day with Mr Craven's Hounds:

Naught was visible save one wretched one-horse close carriage, which in Town is designated a Pill-box, in Paris a Demi-Fortune, and in Brighton a fly—*a lucus a non lucendo,* I suppose. Be its name what it may, it drove up, and out stepped six feet of man, dressed in a shabby scarlet coat, worsted comforter, *dunducketty* mud-covered smalls, with cloth caps to a pair of tremendous, clumsy-looking Wellington boots. This was Mr Craven....I happen to know, as Paul Pry says, that Mr Craven does possess some top-boots....I never saw so many red (or *had been* red) coats with so few top-boots; and some of the wearers looked as if they were going to plough rather than to hunt. Lord Gage and Mr Donovan certainly had the worst clothes....Mr Donovan goes if his horse chooses to run away with him, when he astonishes everyone and no one more than himself...

And the Old Berkeley:

The style in which the hunt is managed is far from pleasant. The members appear to regard strangers as intruders, and there is constant enquiry going on as to who brought such a person out, and

37

whose friend that other is and how a third unfortunate, who appears to have neither friend nor acquaintance, could have found out where they were going to meet...

And here he is on no less a personage than the Duke of Wellington: 'I took off my hat', he says, 'to the greatest man of the day.' His respect, however, ended there for following it came the comment of Surtees, aged twenty-five, on the victor of Waterloo:

The Duke of Wellington, though mighty in the field of war, cuts no great figure hunting. Indeed I have never seen a man with less idea of riding; his seat is unsightly in the extreme, and few men get more falls in the course of a year...

These examples could be multiplied; even when he generalized he let his invective flow, frequently overdoing it just as Nimrod had done at the other extreme in the way of fulsome praise:

The dress fox-hunter is a terrible bore. These people affect watering-places chiefly, though every hunt has one or more of such cattle. They are noisy, rattling, jabbering, rapid blockheads, always on the jab or showing off before women. They are generally great swells; everything of the newest and most approved pattern, from the button on their hats to the spur at their heels. They mostly come up at the last moment just as the Master has exhausted his patience in waiting, and are generally cased in some new-fangled contrivance for keeping clean that which was put on to be dirtied...[1]

No wonder one commentator has remarked that Surtees found it easier to make enemies than friends.

Nimrod's tours, as Mr Watson has put it, were in the nature of stately progresses from mansion to mansion with a stud of horses and a string of servants. Surtees confined himself to one hunter and a hack which he sent on to the various centres he intended to visit, travelling down himself by coach and putting up at the local inn.

The discomforts he endured on these expeditions were terrible and cannot have helped to temper the vitriol which poured from his pen. Once off the main roads or turnpikes where smart turnouts such as The Age on the Brighton run, the Defiance between London and Manchester, or the Holyhead Royal Mail provided reasonable comfort for passengers, the standard of transport was deplorable. The coaches were for the most part draughty, slow, badly sprung and ill-maintained. They were also almost invariably unpunctual and totally incapable, it seemed, of keeping to any set timetable. Mr Jorrocks is surely expressing many of Surtees's own experiences when he is made to say, on the road to Paris:

'Oh, dear! My behind aches as if I had been kicked all the way from Hackleyhole to Marylebone. Are we near Paris? for I'm sure I can't find seat any longer, indeed I can't. I'd rather ride two hundred miles in nine hours like H'osbaldeston, than be shut up in this woiture another hour. It really is past bearing, and that's the long and the short of the matter.

Jorrocks's Jaunts and Jollities, Chapter 9

There was, too, the ever present risk of accident and serious injury caused by drunken coachmen or careless maintenance of the carriage itself. Nimrod recalled a conversation told him by an old-time coachman: '"Jem," a passenger said, "What will you take me to Birmingham for?" "My fare, sir," said I, "is fifteen shillings." "I can go by the Rora (Aurora)," said he, "for ten." "No doubt, sir," I replied, "but then there's the doctor's bill!" He went with me and that very day they had an accident with the Rora.'[2]

With the passengers arrived at their destination they found little relief from the discomforts of the journey if condemned to spend the night, as Surtees was, at the village inn. Most of these were primitive in the extreme; the food was badly cooked and poorly served and often all but inedible, the beer and wine execrable, and the accommodation rudimentary. Nor did proprietor and staff go out of their way to help a solitary stranger of whom they knew nothing, and who carried with him neither the appearance of rank nor the trappings of wealth. Surtees had a rod in pickle for them, too: 'Every slipshod, bloated, red-faced unshaven fellow called a publican (and generally worthy of the name of sinner) who dares to impose . . . so *prenez garde,* my jolly Bonifaces!'

The only alternative to coach travel was the railway, just getting established amidst furious opposition. Country people from the great landlords downwards looked upon railways with much the same suspicion and dread as many regard nuclear power today. It was held that the smoke from engines would pollute the atmosphere and constitute a grave danger to health, that sparks from the engine would set fire to the neighbouring crops (which, on occasion, they did), that the whole thing was an interference with the immemorial rural way of life and, moreover, constituted a legal nuisance. In an endeavour to prove the latter point at law both the Duke of Northumberland and another large landowner living near Hamsterley had attempted to halt the march of progress by applying for injunctions against the railway company. The attempt failed but local and landowning opposition did succeed in re-routing the laying of several portions of the lines to the considerable inconvenience of later generations who sometimes found their local stations situated at a distance from the villages which they served.

As time went on the conveniences offered by the railways came to be appreciated, opposition declined and, as Surtees wrote of one of his characters whose garden was about to be bisected by a new portion of the line, 'Nothing but a strong application of golden ointment could have got over the difficulty. Ten thousand pounds for two thousand pounds worth of property mollified him. The next line of railway had fewer opponents, the third one less and so on in a diminishing ratio.'

Fox-hunting communities all over England were, of course, up in arms against the new mode of transport which, they held, would ruin sport, massacre their hounds, and pollute the air they and their horses breathed. At first Surtees took their part. Railways were, he considered, 'a great nuisance', and as for their coaches, 'their dirty appearance seemed well adapted to the passengers who travel in them'. Later he came to realize their advantages and especially the facilities they offered him for getting about the country on his sporting tours, and he lived to see and accept without regret the universality of railway travel. Indeed, in 1852 under the pseudonym 'An Old Stager', he published a pamphlet entitled *Hints to Railway Travellers and Country Visitors to London.* He was always a conservative but never, in material matters, a hidebound one.

When Surtees was on tour he would have to make his own way to the chosen meet either relying on an inaccurate and ill-drawn map sometimes hung in inn parlours as an assistance to travellers, or on muddled and all but incomprehensible directions from a servant or post-boy or 'chawbacons' encountered on the way. (Nimrod, of course, left a country house on a bloodlike hack accompanied by its Master or a covey of servants to direct him.) The turnpikes were well enough surfaced by the new macadam system, but a journey along them involved frequent and expensive stops at toll-gates. Once away from them, however, conditions became far worse. There were virtually no signposts or finger-posts and the surfaces of the so-called roads or lanes, especially after rain, was virtually non-existent. Mr Sponge's journey to a meet of the Flat Hat Hounds is an accurate account of many of Surtees's own experiences:

With the aid of the groom's instructions, who accompanied him out of the courtyard, Sponge was enabled to set off at a hard canter, cheered by the groom's observation, that 'he thought he would be there in time'. On, on he went; now speculating on a turn; now pulling a scratch map he had made on a bit of paper out of his waistcoat-pocket; now inquiring the name of any place he saw of any person he met. So he proceeded for five or six miles without much difficulty; the road, though not all turnpike, being mainly over good sound township ones. It was at the village of Swineley, with its chubby-towered church and miserable hut-like cottages, that his troubles were to begin. He had two sharp turns to make—to ride through a straw-yard, and leap over a broken-down wall at the corner of a cottage—to get into Swaithing Green Lane, and so cut off an angle of two miles. The road then became a bridle one, and was, like all bridle ones, very plain to those who know them, and very puzzling to those who don't. It was evidently a little-frequented road; and what with looking out for footmarks (now nearly obliterated by the recent rains) and speculating on what queer corners of the fields the gates would be in, Mr Sponge found it necessary to reduce his pace to a very moderate trot.... At last he got through them, and into Red Pool Common, which, by leaving the windmill to the right, he cleared pretty cleverly, and entered a district still wilder and drearier than any he had traversed. Pewits screamed and hovered over land that seemed to grow little but rushes and water-grasses, with occasional heather. The ground poached and splashed as he went ... As he went floundering along through an apparently interminable and almost bottomless lane, whose sunken places and deep ruts were filled with clayey water, which played the very deuce with the cords and brown boots, the light note of a hound fell on his ear ...

Mr Sponge's Sporting Tour, Chapter 20

Nothing was ever lost on Surtees, and he was well served by the mask of anonymity he refused to discard. Since a friend and fellow north-countryman, Frank Sitwell, who had helped him obtain his appointment on the *Sporting Magazine*, was then writing under the name of 'Nim North', he adopted the pseudonym of 'Nim South'. As a result many of the hunts he visited, at least at first, did not know that the stranger in their midst was a sporting journalist ('I did not conceive it necessary to placard myself as a scribbler', he wrote), and he had ample opportunity to gather material for his novels. Mr Sponge himself is mistaken for a distinguished hunting reporter with comic and unforeseen results. The members of the various hunts must have been surprised and taken aback to read the candid comments appearing in the magazine on their turn-out and performances.

Once rumours as to his identity did begin to get about: 'I left people to find it out as best they could—never telling them—at the same time not denying it when asked.'[3] But he did his best to conceal it just the same, informing one correspondent that he was 'noticeably corpulent' when he was, of course, tall and spare, and answering another's totally false imagined description of him, 'You have got me to a T.' It suited him well to preserve his anonymity as long as he could: 'A chiel's amang ye takin' notes, and, faith he'll prent it,' he might well have echoed along with Burns since that, in fact, was just what he was doing.

Consciously or unconsciously he was storing away in that amazing memory of his characters, conversations, scenes, mishaps, and misadventures which were all to reappear, shaped by the artist's hand, later on. Many of the instances and expressions, given such pungent life when emerging from Mr Jorrocks's rubicund lips in his Sportin' Lectors sprang from conversations overheard or exchanged. The famous 'How I wish I was a Heagle, 'overin' over 'em, seein' which 'ound 'as the scent...' was, for instance, inspired by an observation he heard from a Mr Butler, a hunting parson, and one of the few men during those years to earn an encomium from Surtees because 'he rode to hunt, not, like many, hunting to ride'. Mr Butler said to Surtees when hounds were giving cry in some thick, impenetrable Dorsetshire woods that 'he wished he had a balloon in which he could hover over the pack and see what they were all about'.

Mr Butler was, in fact, just the sort of man with whom Surtees found himself in sympathy and whom he could sincerely and readily admire. He was at the homespun heart of rural England where Surtees, too, felt himself to be truly at home. Here there was no pretension, no fuss, no grandeur, but sincerity and true sportsmanship—or so he thought and said. In effect, however, in his revulsion from all that Nimrod stood for he went too far in the opposite direction, denying all good to the Shires and ascribing no faults to the provinces.

He did on occasions on his tours penetrate into Leicestershire but the plain fact was that he was neither a good enough horseman nor a bold enough rider for the Shires. He must have known this and hated it, for there are few men who in their hearts truly despise courage and dash; and when exhibited to a superlative degree by the cracks of the day, most men are envious of it. Being a man who would never admit himself in second place or give way to anyone, he made a virtue of necessity, producing an ingenious explanation for his position in the hunt and at the same time issuing an implied criticism of his predecessor: 'The chronicler of a run', he declared, 'was not expected to ride in front, or how could he tell what was going on behind?'

It is a fact, also, that as yet Surtees's work in journalism his hunting reports and general articles, had shown no trace of the humour, verve, and the feeling for the fun of the thing which were to permeate his best books, especially, of course, *Handley Cross*; he was still learning his trade. He was, at least to some extent, still practising as a solicitor though his attention to the law must have been very limited. His name, however, remained on the Law Society's books as being in practice. He may, of course, have kept it there as an insurance against failure for he was a cautious man, and journalism was an even more hazardous profession than the law. If he did so it must have seemed to him, in the short term at any rate, that the precaution had been a prudent one for his stay with the *Sporting Magazine* was brief, lasting only a little over a year.

The *Sporting Magazine,* as Surtees soon found out, was very scantily staffed. Mr Shury, who had succeeded Pittman as editor, was 'a very respectable and obliging man, but without any sporting knowledge or authority'; Sitwell (Nim North) and a man called Copland who wrote sporadically on hunting in the southern counties under the name of Dashwood and whom Surtees regarded as both idle and useless, were the only two constant contributors besides himself. As a result much of the work in filling the pages devolved on him so that he was compelled to adopt other pseudonyms such as 'A Durham Sportsman', or simply to write and publish unsigned articles. Soon he came to the conclusion that he was being inadequately remunerated for the work he was doing. He also believed that, were he given a free hand, he could manage the magazine much better himself. Accordingly he approached the proprietors with the proposition that he should buy a share in the magazine and become joint editor with Mr Shury.

He was turned down but the proprietors did agree to make a larger contribution towards the cost of his hunting tours.

Surtees then began to find, just as Nimrod had done, that however hard one tried (and Nimrod, of course, had not tried at all) these tours were ruinously expensive. Despite the increased contribution they were costing more than they were worth to him. 'No one who has not tried it', he wrote, 'can have any idea of the cost of hunting touring.' Mr Tilbury charged twelve guineas a month for keeping his horses, 'the gentleman who hires the horse paying keep and all expenses'.[4] The keep he reckoned at a further £2 a week, and travelling from one hunt to another with a groom added even more to his outgoings. Unlike Nimrod, Surtees kept meticulous accounts and he has left on record one bill presented to him by his groom:

PAID AT THE GEORGE INN CRAWLEY
The Day of—1830

1 horse's hay	1/6d
Mash, corn, benes(*sic*)	6/9d
Greasing	Nil
Ostler	1/0.

9/3 + 1/– tip

When totted up these additional sums came to a considerable amount for he was away touring much of the time. The increase granted did not, therefore, he felt, in any way meet the costs he incurred.

There was, too, the expense of mounting himself, for touring was as hard on horses as on men and frequently he had to hire. 'Livery keepers, especially those who let out horses, are often sad rogues,' he was later to write. 'I have known what was called a highly respectable man in London let out an employer's horse for hire when he thought the animal would not be wanted by the owner.' Whether he was referring to Mr Tilbury in this passage is, of course, unknown, but undoubtedly from his experiences came the characters of Peter Leather in *Mr Sponge's Sporting Tour* and Mr Goodheart Green in *Mr Facey Romford's Hounds* who, it may be remembered, was 'a sort of horse-dealing bat, veering between the plaited straw, yellow sand magnificence of Piccadilly and Oxford Street, and the queerly smelling back slum quarters of the check-stealing fly-by-night chaunters and copers . . . he had a happy knack of blending the useless with the dangerous, and was always ready to exchange a low-priced slave for a high-priced savage, or *vice versa*.' (Chapter 12)

After a few months Dashwood retired and the entire burden of keeping the pages filled fell upon him. Irregular and uninspiring though Dashwood's contributions had been they had at least helped to complete the issues in which they appeared. At this time, too, Surtees was trying to put the finishing touches to his legal text-book *The Horseman's Manual*. This was published in 1831 by Alfred Miller of Oxford Street and was a severely technical work. It was also the only book of his ever to be published over his own name. It showed a complete grasp of its subject and demonstrated how well Surtees, however much he disliked it, had mastered his profession.

He had no doubt that, properly managed, the magazine could be made into a valuable commercial property but he was also determined not to lie down any longer under the treatment he was receiving. He enjoyed journalism and touring and did not want to quit the life and return to the law. In consequence he put another proposition to the proprietors, varying the arrangement he had asked for earlier. He now suggested that he should be given a partnership on the following terms: 'The value of the magazine be ascertained, and an interest sufficient to bear his hunting expenses given so long as he continued to write for it, together with a proportionate part of the profits, and on ceasing to write he should have the option of purchasing such share on the valuation so made.'

There is some suggestion that it had been brought to the notice of Mr Pittman's widow who had, it appears, been left the controlling interest in the magazine, that Surtees's candid comments on hunts and huntsmen during his tours were not doing the circulation any good. Mrs Pittman had already played an important part in influencing the decision to sue Nimrod and now she was not anxious to continue with Surtees, at least as long as he remained as hunting correspondent. At all events Surtees received the reply from the proprietors that they 'respectfully but firmly declined admitting any gentleman, however talented, to a share in the magazine'. They did, however, leave the door open for further negotiation and made him an offer which they stated 'was greater than the proprietors ever intended to make, and more than under any circumstances would be made to any other gentleman'.[5]

It was a tempting and probably more than adequate, even generous offer, but in Surtees's eyes it was not enough and his hackles rose immediately. He could never either compromise or chaffer except perhaps—and this only occasionally—over a horse. He reacted exactly in the manner for which he had criticized Nimrod. He resigned. But, unlike Nimrod, he was not in debt to the paper and he had taken steps to cover his retreat.

He did not forsake journalism. It is all but certain that, anticipating the result of his request for a partnership, he had already been negotiating with Rudolph Ackermann junior, the fine art publisher, with a view to starting a new sporting paper. They agreed terms in February 1831 almost as soon as Surtees's resignation took effect, and the first issue of the *New Sporting Magazine* appeared only two months later, in May, with Surtees installed as editor and hunting correspondent.

From the first Ackermann appears to have given Surtees a free hand and the paper prospered. A friendship ripened between the two men which lasted until they fell out a year or so later.

The Ackermann business had been founded by Rudolph

Ackermann senior, father of Surtees's backer. He had been born at Stolberg in Germany where his father had been a coach-builder. He himself had many talents including engraving, painting, and coach designing. He had settled in London in the 1790s, marrying an Englishwoman and producing designs for the principal coach-builders. So successful was he that he had been entrusted with the designs for Lord Nelson's funeral coach. A man of many talents, he produced patents for movable carriage axles, and he is credited with establishing lithography in England as a fine art. Later in his career he became a publisher and was responsible for *Ackermann's Poetical Magazine* and the *Repository of Arts, Literature, Fashions, Manufactures etc* which appeared in forty volumes made up from monthly parts costing 3*s*. 6*d*. When he suffered a stroke in 1830 his son, Rudolph, took over the business, turning the fine art side more and more towards sporting subjects.

The *New Sporting Magazine* was an immediate and outstanding success for Surtees, who proved himself to be a gifted and hard-working editor, and gathered about him a formidable body of expert contributors. In doing so he did not hesitate to poach from his former employers. Dashwood had left the other magazine saying of its proprietors that 'no man with the feelings of a gentleman could have anything to do with them' but when he heard of Surtees's departure he had, nevertheless, thoughts of returning. Learning of this Surtees snapped him up immediately. He neither liked Dashwood nor admired his work but he was determined to do everything in his power to make the new venture a success and in the process injure the board of the 'old' *Sporting,* as it came to be called, by showing its members what they had lost in letting him go. Dashwood was not much addition to the new venture but, as Surtees said 'if he did not strengthen us much, at all events weakened them'. Another occasional contributor to the 'old' *Sporting* was Dicky Lawrence who wrote on veterinary subjects. Surtees lost no time in recruiting him, too, into his ranks.

But it was in capturing the illustrators that he hit the old magazine hardest. One of his first contributors was Francis

Grant, a lifelong friend who later became President of the Royal Academy and gained a knighthood. Grant had sporting tastes; he, too, had abandoned the law, in his case for painting. Although largely self-taught he soon made a name. His group 'Queen Victoria and Lord Melbourne Riding in Windsor Park' was such a fashionable success that he became the most sought-after portrait painter of the day. Where he went others followed. Ackermann, too, with his sporting connections helped to bring in artists. As well as Grant, Abraham Cooper was Surtees's big catch. Like Grant he was largely self-taught, and an Academician of considerable standing and influence. 'Though shooting was his forte,' Surtees says, 'he could do hunting subjects extremely well and his battle pieces were considered masterpieces.'[6] Cooper brought with him Webb, one of the most skilled engravers of his time, who until his untimely death was of inestimable value to Surtees.

In Cooper's wake came J. F. Herring, who had been a professional coachman before he exchanged his whip for a brush, and who had studied under Cooper. Henry Bernard Chalon, another Academician, all but forgotten now but much admired then and a favourite of the Royal family, was another who brought distinction to his pages; and Sir Edwin Landseer was another contributor, of whom Surtees had no very high opinion. He published Landseer's illustrations, he said, 'for the sake of the name' for they were, he thought 'mere make-weights'. There was something in what he said for the prettiness and sentimentality of Landseer's drawings accorded ill with the more virile work of his other illustrators and, as Surtees had to point out to one of them whose preferred drawings were landscapes and such things as chamois-hunting in the Alps, he was 'catering for gentlemen whose continued cry was, "Give us horses! horses, nothing but horses!"'

Surtees has been called both vindictive and unscrupulous in enticing away the best contributors and illustrators from his former employers and to some extent these accusations are true. But it was always his way to give back two blows for one received, and he felt he had been hard done by at the hands of the proprietors of the 'old' *Sporting* considering all the work and indeed money he had put into their publication whilst he had worked for it. It has to be remembered, too, that he was still the younger son making his way in the world without any prospects or unearned resources. Failure now would mean being thrown back on the law and he must have felt that this alone entitled him to fight for the present and future existence of the new magazine with any weapons at his command.

Quite apart from these personal feelings proprietary journalism has always been a ruthless trade and besides, the contributors to the old magazine would hardly have come to him had they felt any dedicated loyalty to it, for he could offer them neither better terms nor a substantial increase in salary. Mrs Pittman, her partners, and advisers were a hard, unsparing, predatory lot; 'incompetent, stingy and obstinate' was how Surtees described them and, as their future conduct was to show, such adjectives were abundantly justified.

Surtees failed to attract Ruff, the greatest racing expert of his day and the founder of *Ruff's Guide to the Turf,* so he employed instead Hamilton Reynolds as racing correspondent. Reynolds was introduced to him by the Honourable Fitzroy Stanhope, who was well known in both the racing and literary worlds. All his life Surtees hated racing but he knew that he had to have the sport well and accurately covered in order to please his readership. Reynolds's knowledge and literary talents were more than adequate, but he was idle and needed driving. His manuscript 'would be delivered in the most extraordinary state of confusion—scribbled on letter-backs, old play-bills, anything he could get hold of—written in a hand that seemed impossible to decipher. After several attempts to read it I was obliged to give it to the printer, with, I confess, no great expectation of its merit. Most agreeably surprised I was to find it read so well. Hamilton Reynolds was a very clever fellow.'[7]

Colonel Peter Hawker, one of the finest game-shots of the day, the 'father of wild-fowling' and author of the classic

Instructions to Young Sportsmen in all that Relates to Game and Shooting gave his expert advice and lent his authority to the shooting pages, and W. H. Maxwell, author of the Irish sporting classic *Wild Sports of the West* was also a frequent contributor. Another to write for him was Grantley Berkeley, the violent and eccentric sporting squire who was the author of several historical novels after the manner of Sir Walter Scott, and a pamphleteer in support of game-laws and blood sports, later author of the famous *Reminiscences of a Huntsman*.

They were not an easy team to manage, every one of them being headstrong, pugnacious, and independent. Hawker, whilst indulging in his passion for wild-fowling which he described as 'an odd mixture of ecstasy and slavery', was almost as quick to threaten his fowling-piece on those who interrupted his sport or disturbed his prey as Colonel Charrittie had been; Grantley Berkeley, on reading an adverse review of his first novel *Berkeley Castle* in *Fraser's Magazine* had fought a duel with the reviewer, Maginn, and horse-whipped the magazine's editor, thus provoking the *mot* that went round fashionable London: 'If Fraser's might be called the cream of periodicals, it was more accurately described as *whipped* cream.'

In his endeavours to attract famous names to his pages Surtees went to the lengths of writing to James Hogg, the shepherd from Ettrick Forest whose early attempts at poetry had been discovered and fostered by Sir Walter Scott, asking him for an article on fishing. Hogg, whose name had been made with the publication of 'The Queen's Wake', a long poem on Mary Queen of Scots, and who now mixed with the literary great (he had considerable influence on Robert Louis Stevenson amongst others) was perplexed by the request for he had never heard of either Surtees or the magazine, and he took his time about replying. When eventually Hogg, who in his private life was a heavy drinker and in his literary one a hard hitter in the manner of the day, did reply he confessed his total ignorance of Surtees: 'But if you are either my old friend Mainsforth or any near relation of his I will write for you for nothing with all the pleasure in the world. Otherwise I will always take pay and warrant any man an ass who doesn't.'[8] But the effort to enlist him as a contributor failed just the same and nothing appeared over his signature in the *New Sporting*.

Surtees was now beginning to mix outside the circles of law and fox-hunting in which he had hitherto moved and to penetrate the fringes of the literary world. One of the most interesting acquaintanceships he then made and one which ripened into a lasting friendship was with Mark Lemon, the future editor of *Punch* and *The Field*. Lemon came from a Jewish family of humble origins and his parents were victuallers in a small way. He had literary aspirations and ambitions as a dramatist. Those of his plays which were put on were, however, failures, and at the time when Surtees met him he was twenty-two years old and trying to make his way as a journalist. Under the name of Tom Moody he wrote some 'very clever semi-sporting sketches' for the *New Sporting* which Surtees eagerly accepted. As a writer Lemon was a hack but he had a talent for friendship and amongst his acquaintances was W. M. Thackeray, then also anxious to make his name as a writer and editing for his step-father the *National Standard and Journal of Literature, Science, Music and the Fine Arts*. Although the friendship between Thackeray and Surtees did not mature until much later it is probable that it was Lemon who first brought Surtees to Thackeray's notice during that time in London. Thackeray always preferred sporting, active types to literary men and Surtees's tastes, background, and knowledge of sporting lore would all have appealed to him.

Such were some of the galaxy of contributors Surtees gathered about him to make the magazine into the success it was. But there was one name lacking from his list and, whatever his personal feeling for him, it was a name Surtees badly wanted to add to it—the name of Nimrod.

Nimrod himself, now moved from the town of Calais to a château on the Dunkirk road, was, in exile, most unwilling to lay down his pen. Having realized his error in leaving the 'old'

Sporting he was anxious to repair it and to retrieve the position he had once held. As well as he was able he was keeping in touch with the sporting-literary world of London and he wanted to return to it. Nor had he been forgotten. Before he had left the 'old' *Sporting* his limpid style and the erudition of his articles had attracted the attention of the literary editor of the *Morning Post* who had written of him as 'a gentleman who appeared to have passed half his life among hounds, horses and coachmen, and whose style was so excellent that it was a pity it had not been more worthily directed'.[9] This, in turn, brought him to the notice of J. G. Lockhart, the future biographer of Scott and the editor of the weighty and influential *Quarterly Review*.

John Gibson Lockhart was to play an important part in the lives and literary careers of both Nimrod and Surtees. He was a Scot, the son of a parson who gave him a most rigorous upbringing and inflicted upon him a lonely and unhappy childhood. He was also congenitally deaf in one ear. These two things combined with an over-sensitive nature to give him a grudge against the world. From Glasgow High School he obtained an exhibition to Balliol where he did well. On coming down from Oxford he wrote two novels which failed to find a publisher; he then studied for and was called to the Bar but found no briefs forthcoming when he commenced to practise.

These failures increased a natural tendency towards misanthrophy engendered by his upbringing and physical handicap. More or less by chance he fell in with John Wilson who wrote under the name of Christopher North and who combined a talent for invective with the ability to express it in print in the most biting and virulent terms. Together they became the principal and controlling contributors to *Blackwood's Magazine* which they made notorious for its attacks on almost everyone of note in the literary world. One of Sir Walter Scott's biographers describes it at that time as 'Libellous, defamatory, scurrilous, malicious, ferocious, blackguardly, caddish and mostly childish'.[10] Childish or not it was successful, effective, and horribly wounding.

When Lockhart fell in love with Scott's daughter, Sophia, and wanted to marry her, his renown as a destroyer of literary reputations caused Scott to have serious reservations as to the suitability of the match. Lockhart, however, who was in appearance a singularly handsome man who could exercise great charm when he wished, succeeded in the end in banishing his prospective father-in-law's doubts. In time, too, Scott came to perceive the trueness of the talent underlying the scurrility, he consented, and the marriage took place.

Scott attempted to put a halt to the poison emanating from Lockhart's pen and to an extent he succeeded but not before an extraordinary affair of literary animosities had almost involved Lockhart in a duel. The affair ended in Lockhart's friend and prospective second, Jonathan Christie, becoming so personally involved that he had to fight the calumniator himself. Christie killed his man and was lucky to escape with his life in the subsequent trial for murder.

Lockhart promised his father-in-law to abandon forever the gutter journalism of *Blackwood's* and in 1823, through the influence of Scott, he went to London to edit for the publisher John Murray a new literary-cum-political magazine to be called the *Quarterly Review*. Under his guidance the *Quarterly*, as it came to be known, prospered and through it he wielded immense influence on the literary life of the time. A review in the *Quarterly* could make or, more usually, break, a book by any writer established or otherwise. For Lockhart had not entirely put aside his venomous attacks and still produced some of the clever, erudite, but savagely hostile reviews of books he disliked or of which he thought little. But, arrogant and aloof though he appeared to many, Lockhart could be a true friend to those who were allowed to penetrate behind his unforthcoming and austere exterior. He was, too, by any standards, a great editor, keenly alive to the literary and political issues of the day, always eager to spot new talent and open and broadminded in his approach to subject-matter,

R.S. Surtees. Portrait formerly hanging in Hamsterley Hall, Co. Durham

Nimrod (Charles James Apperley). Engraving

ready and anxious to recognize literary ability from whatever unlikely corner it appeared to spring.

Surtees became aware of the interest in Nimrod that was being displayed in more literary circles than his own. Although he detested Nimrod's high-falutin' notions and his general attitude to sport he recognized his value as a commercial property and the *réclame* his name and style would bring to the new magazine could he secure his services for it. But he had also learnt of the embargo placed on the use of the name 'Nimrod' other than in the 'old' *Sporting* for a period of ten years. He, too, had had experience of the vengeful nature of Mr Pittman's widow. He did not care about women much, anyway, anywhere and above all in business. Years later he was to make his sole sympathetic female character, Lucy Glitters, say that the only compensation she had for being a woman was that she did not have to marry one. His comment on Mrs Pittman's behaviour in the conduct of the magazine and her negotiations with Nimrod was all of a piece with his general low opinion of her sex: 'Mr Pittman showed his sense by keeping the matter to himself, for a woman's place is in her own home and not her husband's counting-house; and had Mr Pittman been equally judicious in the disposition of his property the present question would not have arisen.'

Nimrod himself thought the new venture bound to fail. He knew nothing of Surtees personally, nor does he seem to have been aware that it was Surtees who had succeeded him as hunting correspondent, for Surtees, as we have seen, was expert in covering his tracks. He did not think that there was room for a further sporting paper and, swallowing his pride, he applied to the 'old' *Sporting* for his former job back again. He was met with an adamant refusal and in this Mrs Pittman, or whoever made the decision, was probably wise for nothing could stop Nimrod's extravagances once he sat on a horse or went to a meet. He was also given a sharp reminder of his obligations under the agreement which precluded the use of his name elsewhere.

Nevertheless Lockhart wanted him for the *Quarterly* and

wrote to him suggesting a series of articles dealing with aspects of sporting life. This was an entirely new departure for the *Quarterly* and Lockhart believed it would breathe some fresh air into its normally staid pages. Surtees also wanted him but, knowing Lockhart's interest, with typical shrewdness he held his hand so that if any action were to be taken by the 'old' *Sporting* it would be against the *Quarterly,* not him. The *Quarterly,* published and backed by Murray, Byron's friend and publisher, and edited by Lockhart, had far greater resources to meet a lawsuit or fight an injunction than had Surtees's fledgling.

Having been turned down by the 'old' *Sporting* Nimrod had in fact written to its competitor, and in passing it is worth noting that there is none of the bombast or self-advertisement of which he is so often accused and which, if it was endemic to him, might have been expected to appear in this application for employment:

SIR,

You will much oblige me by informing me, by return of post, whether you will allow me to occupy three or four pages of your opening number. If you can do so, you shall hear further from me on Friday morning.

Yours etc,

CHARLES APPERLEY.

But Surtees, though he badly wanted him, was content to bide his time. 'Nimrod was the King of Diamonds,' he wrote, 'and though we might not get him at first deal, we knew he was in the pack and would come to us at last.'

Meanwhile for Nimrod there was the golden opportunity and great compliment of the articles for the *Quarterly,* for neither Lockhart nor Murray was impressed by the possibility of an action against them by the owners of the 'old' *Sporting.* They asked Nimrod to go ahead; they did, however, agree that the articles should appear unsigned and not over his pseudonym.

Accordingly Nimrod sat down and produced his first article. Unfortunately, writing as he thought for a more cultivated and cultured audience than he had heretofore addressed, he pitched his sights too high, adopting his most affected and artificial style and interlarding almost every sentence with classical quotations. Having read the article Lockhart returned it as unsuitable, and Surtees later commented on it in his most sarcastic vein: 'He proceeded to air Lycurgus, the Spartans, the Persians, and ancient Greeks with a touch of Xenophon, Alexander the Great, Ulysses, Hannibal, Ralph Lambton, Osbaldeston, Cicero, and I don't know who else besides.'[11]

He was not above publishing it himself, however, when the article came to him. It was the first of Nimrod's contributions to appear in the *New Sporting* and was published in four parts under the title of 'The Antiquity and Advantages of Field Sports'. The first part appeared in the issue of January 1832, when the threat of an injunction had largely disappeared.

Despite the fact that he had not cared for Nimrod's initial effort Lockhart still believed in him and wanted something from his pen. He suggested a simpler approach harking back to Nimrod's earlier accounts of hunts and hunting. Nimrod took the advice to heart; he tried again and this time produced one of the classics of sporting literature. 'The Chace, an account of a meet and a hunt across High Leicestershire with the Quorn Hounds', was published anonymously in the *Quarterly* for March 1832. It was a sensational success. A few country rectors and clergymen wrote to the editor protesting that he was letting down the tone of the paper by publishing an essay on a frivolous sport pursued by the uncaring and dissolute rich, but they were in the minority and Lockhart maintained that he could show from his correspondence that their bishops did not support them!

At first the authorship of the article was attributed to Lord Alvanley, but soon its true progenitor was recognized. 'Either the devil or Nimrod wrote this!' was the exclamation of one sporting peer on reading it in White's.

The general recognition of Nimrod's name as a contributor to the *Quarterly* led to a further increase in his fame and reputation and brought him to the notice of a much wider readership than the purely sporting. It was a small-minded act of Surtees, probably inspired by envy, to sneer at the rejected article at the same time as he was publishing it and to hint that Nimrod himself could not unaided have produced such a polished piece of writing as 'The Chace'. The true author, Surtees suggested, was in all probability Lockhart himself. Lockhart may well have edited and tidied the piece for publication but he could not and did not have the knowledge of fox-hunting nor the acquaintanceship with the characters to have been responsible for its authorship; in any event the whole essay bears the unmistakable hallmarks of Nimrod's individual style, as indeed Surtees eventually came to admit in his unpublished notes for an autobiography.[12]

Knowledge of its authorship soon came to the ears of the proprietors of the 'old' *Sporting* who immediately threatened proceedings. Lockhart kept his nerve and replied that since the name 'Nimrod' had not been used they had no cause for action. The proprietors must have realized the strength of this argument for they took the matter no further; they did, however, refuse an offer of £100 to buy out the embargo. Mrs Pittman and her advisers were being vindictive to the last.

Encouraged by their failure to pursue the action Surtees now felt that he could safely employ Nimrod, though his articles would have to be published anonymously or under another name. Since his readership would immediately recognize his style this should not matter very much. Nimrod was taken on and Surtees, though he liked neither the man nor his matter, could now congratulate himself that he held the 'King of Diamonds' of sporting literature in his hand.

Before the first number of the magazine was due to come off the press Surtees's prospects and circumstances took a totally unexpected turn for the better. His elder brother, Anthony, went on a Grand Tour in the winter of 1830 with Sir Benjamin Leighton, a family friend. They decided to continue the tour beyond its usual limits and to explore the East. In

November of that year Anthony wrote to Robert from Jerusalem describing his adventures:

Take an atlas and trace out the following places in Syria; you will then know where your affectionate brother has been travelling—Tripoli, Balbec, Damascus, Bairout, Sidon, Tyre, Aere, Nazareth, Sea of Tiberias, Jaffa, Ramla, Jerusalem. We are here for a few days only...My movements after that must be determined by the governor's generosity. I have written to him for money.... Perhaps I may hear from you at Malta.

To that letter he added a postscript later in the month: 'I am almost shaken to death for the last eight days on a camel across the desert. It was no joke, I assure you.... Till I return—adieu.'[13]

But he never did return. Between Alexandria and Malta on the voyage home he was struck down by smallpox. It was a serious attack and there was then, of course, no known remedy. Put ashore at Malta on 22 March 1831 he died two days later.

Thus, at a stroke, everything was changed for Surtees. Though he was not yet independent, independence was just round the corner. He was the heir to Hamsterley, a man with prospects and a person of some consequence, at least in the north. It did not soften him towards the human race in general nor towards those whom he particularly disliked. Indeed, since he had now less to fear from the consequences, in certain cases it added acid to his pen. But it did in some extraordinary way open his mind. Security or the thought of it unlocked his comic muse. A shaft of sunlight came in to illuminate hitherto hidden and unsuspected sources of fun. Thus John Jorrocks, grocer and future Master of the Handley Cross Foxhounds, was born.

CHAPTER FIVE

Jaunts and Jollities and the End of Editing

JORROCKS did not spring fully fledged from his creator's mind to emerge in all his splendid comic maturity in *Handley Cross*. Far from it. He made his first appearance in the third number of the *New Sporting*, in a piece entitled 'A Day with the Surrey', 'Precisely', as Surtees recalled, 'as the original made it to me out hunting with these hounds.' But he never revealed who the original was beyond describing how he found the actual physical model:

All at once my astonished eyes were confounded by the appearance of a man in a huge antique red frock-coat with a dark collar, mother-o'-pearl buttons with black foxes engraved or painted on them.... The wearer (who I at first took for a mounted general postman) was on a most becoming steed with a snaffle bridle in his mouth decorated with a noseband and an ivory ring under his jaws to keep the reins together; the saddle was brand new and in his right hand he clenched the iron handle of a most tremendous horse-whip ... the horseman had pulled up by my side ere I recognised the friendly features of my old friend Jorrocks.

New Sporting Magazine, July 1831

The articles and sketches describing the adventures and misadventures of Jorrocks and his entourage appeared at intervals in the *New Sporting* between the years 1831 and 1834. They were printed over the pseudonym of 'A Yorkshireman', a pen-name also used by Surtees for other material written by him for the magazine. Throughout the series the 'Yorkshire-man' is introduced as Jorrocks's Boswell and foil. He is young and indigent and, as he says himself, he 'provided the company while Jorrocks provided the cash'. His name is given as Charley Stubbs. He reappears in *Handley Cross,* as transmogrified into 'Stobbs' by the changing of one letter and still employing the catch phrase, 'I'll find the company and you find the cash', for Surtees was never averse to plagiarizing himself when occasion offered. Stubbs or Stobbs was, of course, Surtees himself and one can only speculate once more on what gamey adventures he and that unnamed original got up to during his unregenerate early days in London. Throughout the books there are the strongest possible hints of a more than nodding acquaintance with the seamier side of London life; at this date one did not have to stray far from the principal throughfares to find it. Because of his first-hand knowledge of the hells where dog-fighting and animal-baiting were carried on he sturdily barred all mention of them from the new magazine, nor would he tolerate any reference to cock-fighting.

'Slender Billy', the proprietor of the 'hell' to whom Jorrocks introduced Stobbs, was a real character in every sense of the word. Amongst his other accomplishments he numbered illicit distilling and counterfeiting. Once when revenue officers were about to raid his premises he set his bears on them and put them to rout. He was also strongly suspected of throwing an exciseman who was about to expose his operations into a boiling still. Finally caught with bundles of counterfeit notes in his possession, he ended his short career on the scaffold. His last words were said to have been, 'I dare not now deny it. *I did boil the exciseman.'* Long after Surtees had retired from the *New Sporting* to Hamsterley and respectability he received a letter from his successor in the editorial chair telling him of Slender Billy's subsequent career and sad end, some of which material he incorporated into *Handley Cross*.

In the early sketches in which Jorrocks appeared he is seen through Surtees's eyes as both comic and absurd. He is very far from having attained to the position and rank of MFH which gave dignity to his excesses. The affection for his favourite character which runs right through *Handley Cross* had not yet crept in to temper Surtees's thinly veiled disdain for the ridiculous figure he is made to cut. He is a cockney, 'a cit rapturously fond of sport', 'a substantial grocer in St Botolph's Lane with an elegant residence in Great Coram Street', and, it may be added, a wife he doesn't like and cannot think why he married. She it is who provides the reason for the ruses he has recourse to in order to rid himself of her company and go off on escapades with the 'Yorkshireman'.

But, despite all this, Jorrocks often speaks with the authentic voice of the great man we know and love and one can sometimes see coming into flower for the first time the comedy, the fun, and the sheer exuberance that Surtees had so far concealed:

'Punctuality is the politeness of princes', said Mr Jorrocks, raising a broad-brimmed, lowish-crowned hat, as high as a green hunting-cord which tackled it to his yellow waistcoat with a fox's tooth would allow, as he came upon the Yorkshireman at the corner. 'My soul's on fire and eager for the chase! By heavens, I declare I've dreamt of nothing else all night, and the worst of it is that in a par-ox-ism of delight, when I thought I saw the darlings running into the warmint, I brought Mrs J—— such a dig in the side as knocked her out of bed, and she *swears* she'll go to Jenner and the court for the protection of injured *ribs!* But come—jump up—where's your nag? Binjimin, you blackguard, where are you? The fog is blinding me, I declare! Binjimin, I say! Binjimin! you willain, where are you?'

Jorrocks's Jaunts and Jollities, Chapter 2

But this was Jorrocks on a hunting morning, when he was always at his best. In the sketches Surtees led him through all sorts of other places, Margate, Brighton, Paris, racing in the Bois de Boulogne, flirting with a French countess, in all of which he is hopelessly out of place and out of character and is, as Mr Watson says, frankly a great bore. Jorrocks was only himself and only comes truly alive on the hunting field or near it, with his beloved hounds, talking about (or lecturing on) hunting or rioting with his hunt servants or sporting friends.

There is, in fact, precious little hunting in the *Jaunts and Jollities* as the collected sketches were to be called when published in book form. What there is relates to the Surrey

62

packs with whom Surtees hunted in his early days and with whom Mr Jorrocks, grocer and 'London cit', would naturally have gone out. (He carries a telescope in his pocket the better to survey hounds working. This was mercifully dropped from his repertoire later on.)

In his description of Surrey hunting Surtees could not resist applying the rod in his usual fashion and castigating his old friends who had provided him with his first escape from the drudgery of the law during those years before he found his *métier* in journalism. In his opinion they were not sufficiently single-minded as sportsmen. 'City cits' on their day out, their thoughts were occupied with other things besides the workings of hounds and the pursuit of the fox:

A gentle breeze wafted divers scraps of conversation to his [the Yorkshireman's] ear. What sport had you on Wednesday? No. Is it a likely find today? No, no, no; it was not where the hounds, but what consols, left off at; what the four per cents, and not the four horses, were up to; what the position of the money, not the horse market. 'Anything doing in Danish bonds, sir?' said one. 'You must do it by lease and release and levy a fine', replied another. Scott v Brown, crim con. to be heard on or before Wednesday next.—Barley thirty-two to forty-two....*

Jorrocks's Jaunts and Jollities, Chapter 2

Surtees returns to this charge in 'The Swell and the Surrey' another of the sketches. (One of the weaknesses he showed throughout his writing career was to overstate his case and to belabour his prejudices, as indeed his treatment of Nimrod demonstrates): 'The members of the Surrey are the people who combine business with pleasure, and even in the severest run can find time for sweet discourse, and talk about the price of stocks or stockings. "Yooi wind him there, good dog, yooi wind him."—"Cottons is fell." "Hark to Cottager! Hark!"—"Take your bill at three months..."'

* Oddly enough A.G. Macdonnell in his satire *England Their England* published in 1933 makes an almost exactly identical comment on a smart meet in the Thirties. He can hardly consciously have borrowed from Surtees.

'The Swell' article as a whole is a gentle satire demonstrating what happens when a Melton 'swell' visits the Surrey Hounds with the intention of showing the Provincials how to go and how a country should be crossed and instead meets the nemesis awaiting one who mounts himself on a blood horse in a trappy country.

Surtees himself admitted that the sketch was a parody on Nimrod's famous *Quarterly* article with the priorities reversed in that this time it was the provincials and the snobs who had the last laugh. From this it has been suggested that 'the swell' was Nimrod himself and the article yet another of Surtees's spiteful attacks on him. For once in his relations with Nimrod this is unfair to Surtees. In the first place the swell is portrayed as covered in moustaches while Nimrod was, and always remained, clean-shaven but, secondly and much more tellingly, Surtees, who was never one to disavow an insult or disown the intent to wound, never claimed it as such. Nimrod's speech at Jorrocks's dinner-party later on in the series has also been held up as unkind and derisory. This, again, is unfair and mistaken, for the speech is very short and contains only the gentlest of parodies to which no one could object. Indeed Mr Jorrocks goes out of his way to compliment his distinguished guest, albeit in some confusion caused by downing bumpers of port—

After a pause during which his cheeks twice changed colour, from red to green, and back to red, he again called for a bumper toast, which he prefaced with the following speech, or parts of a speech: 'Gentlemen—in rising—propose toast about to give—feel werry...werry sinsible—great compliment—eyes of England upon us—give you the health—Mr Happerley Nimrod—three times three!'

He then attempted to rise for the purpose of marking the time, but his legs deserted his body, and after two or three lurches, down he went with a tremendous thump under the table. He called first for 'Batsay', then for 'Binjimin', and, game to the last, blurted out, 'Lift me up!—tie me in my chair!—fill my glass!'

Jorrocks's Jaunts and Jollities, Chapter 12

As it happened Nimrod could well afford to shrug off such gentle jibes for with the publication of his *Quarterly* article on 'The Chace', fortune was again smiling on him. *Fraser's Magazine,* the *New Monthly,* even the *Encyclopaedia Britannica* pressed him for contributions. And the *Saturday Magazine* asked him for an article on fox-hunting 'seasoned here and there with a dash of morality'. At first, however, having failed with the old magazine, his main aim and ambition was to resume his sporting tours with the *New Sporting.* But Surtees, wisely, would have none of this. Like the proprietors of the old magazine he knew and dreaded Nimrod's extravagances which his hurried departure and residence in France had done nothing to curb. 'Nimrod', he wrote, 'had no idea of not having everything he wanted and this, too, regardless of expense.' And in this instance he was absolutely right.

Despite all the hardships and the expense, Surtees had enjoyed his own sporting tours and he resolved to continue them. Besides he was now the heir and could look forward with some confidence to 'the governor's generosity' of which his elder brother had before been the sole beneficiary. He set up a stud of his own and he and Herbert Langham of Cottesbroke Park went shares in the hire of five hunters, though the choice of Langham as a partner was a strange one for he was another extravagant squire. The Cottesbroke estate was, in fact, shortly to be administered by the Commissioners in Lunacy after Sir James Langham, the incumbent, had been declared insane. His knowledge of this enquiry may, just possibly, have given Surtees the idea and background for the proceedings where poor Jorrocks is impugned as insane in *Handley Cross.*

The fact that he was now the heir meant, too, that he would not have to continue his life in journalism for ever, nor did he intend to. 'Editing is very good fun for a time. It brings one acquaintance with a variety of—', he left as one of a number of disconnected jottings discovered amongst his papers after his death.[1] He never completed the sentence but it is clear that he regarded his time as editor as an interim period in his life and as a means of enlarging his knowledge of human nature. His ambitions were turning towards the writing of novels and publication in hard covers. The hunting tours, apart from the enjoyment to be derived from them, would help fulfil that purpose. He must have known that as a prospective novelist it was necessary to expand his horizons, and on these tours he was constantly exploring new backgrounds, meeting fresh faces, and encountering different characters. Many of these acquaintances subsequently appeared in fictional form, not well enough disguised to prevent recognition or to increase his popularity.

But he still took care on these tours to preserve his anonymity as best he could. Not one of the hunting reports or articles that appeared in the *New Sporting* was signed by him; he even concealed from his grooms that he was a 'magazine man' or 'book man' as hunting reporters were beginning to be called, and he felt himself complimented when told he looked like neither.

When he set out on his second series of tours in the winter of 1831 a fresh peril was added to the discomforts of the road. There was at that time considerable agrarian unrest and riots had broken out. The labourers feared that new machinery would take away their livelihood. They demonstrated violently against any change from traditional methods of farming, occasionally taking possession of farms by force and smashing the machinery. In addition there was agitation and rioting over the Reform Bill, and an outbreak of cholera morbus which, from its first appearance in October 1831, swept through most of the country. Lawless bands of displaced workmen and wreckers roamed the countryside pillaging and looting and leaving a trail of destruction in their wake. As a stranger whose identity and occupation were unknown and who was secretive about both, Surtees was at times at risk both from the marauders who feared he was a government agent and from the authorities who suspected him of being an agitator in disguise.

None of this prevented him from making his progress through the counties though at times now he did stay with the great in their country houses or mansions, paying a visit to Grantley Berkeley at Berkeley Castle and Squire Osbaldeston 'who hunted Leicestershire in a style that it had never been hunted before, and never has since'. These were exceptions, for mostly he continued his practice of staying at inns whose standards of comfort he continued to castigate. Although he considered 'broiled ham and tea' the best of breakfasts on a hunting morning, he could never get it on time from the slovenly servants, and as for the port he was offered with his victuals when he returned after a hard day: 'What wretched stuff many of them put before their guests in the name of port, sometimes so bad it is not even drinkable when put into negus, and most of them retain a third of the bottle to put into a pint for somebody else.' Nor did his comments on hunts and huntsmen become any less acerbic than heretofore and he did not hesitate to name names: 'I cannot compliment Weaver on his proficiency as a huntsman, neither can I say much for his whipper-in who, in addition to other good qualities, is nearly as deaf as a post. Weaver does not seem to know that it is his business to be with his hounds . . .'; 'Mr Sullivan, a young man, carried a horn (which he could not blow) slung over his shoulder . . .'; 'It is unsufferable to think that Melton is the only place worth hunting from and a great deal of this second horse business is all flash and humbug . . .'

On the other hand, on the very rare occasions when he found someone he could and did wholeheartedly admire, he could be almost as fulsome as Nimrod. Here he is on Major Wyndham of the Scots Greys:

He is always in his place, never distressing his horse, never riding for a sprint spurt, or jumping for jumping's sake, but going steadily, just doing what is necessary and no more, and I will be bound for it that Major Wyndham sees more of hounds and knows more of the ins and outs of each run than two-thirds of the 10st men who are out. Moreover he is not one of your fine talking men who, because he has hunted in Leicestershire d—s all provincials, and turns up his nose when he comes to the plough. In fact he is a fine specimen of a soldier, a sportsman, and a polished gentleman.

None of his cutting comments stopped the success of the magazine or impaired its circulation. As he said himself when he referred to them and to the easily recognizable characters who lay behind the caricatures in his books: 'Most men take a pleasure in satire when it is not directed at themselves'.[2] He was never one to underestimate the weaknesses of human nature nor to avoid playing on them, and he was, as usual when he was at his most cynical, absolutely right as other publications containing uninhibited revelations and reflections have demonstrated down the years. There were many who must have purchased the paper half in dread of their own names appearing, but also with a lively expectation of relishing what was said about others.

In addition to his own work the magazine owed much of its success to his excellence as an editor, for he had an unerring eye for talent and what was likely to please the public, culled from encounters on his hunting tours. And he was dedicated to his task; he was a tireless traveller and indefatigable worker, always ready to fill in himself if a contributor was late or failed to produce his copy.

But there remained the problem of what to do with Nimrod now that he had got him. Surtees was fully alive to his importance as a writer on hunting and knew, too, that neither his name nor his reputation had been forgotten. When reconsidering his earlier hunting reports he paid him a tribute that was for once unreserved and unqualified:

Nimrod was a good English writer. We have heard that one of the greatest authorities of the day pronounced him one of the best writers we had. This power, applied to a subject in which he was heart and soul, of course produced corresponding success. Nothing can be better, more sporting, dashing or characteristic than his hunting contributions to the *Sporting Magazine.* These papers may be read and enjoyed by persons who never saw a hound.[3]

Thinking over these past successes he hit upon the happy idea of asking Nimrod to write a series on 'Characters of the

Hunting Countries'. It was a subject admirably suited to Nimrod's talents. He immediately agreed and from the first the articles, though unsigned, were recognized as coming from his hand. Surtees himself went to the extent of describing them as 'very masterly' though here, typically, he qualified the compliment by averring that Nimrod was in fact only working over again the material he had gleaned from his former hunting tours. The articles, he said, were, 'the lake of the tour drawn off in streams'. He could never remain impartial or generous towards Nimrod for very long. Whatever private reservations he may have had, however, it remained a fact that Nimrod's name, though unpublicized, his articles, and his skills added greatly to the reputation and circulation of the magazine.

It must be confessed, too, that Surtees had some reason to be irritated with his new and celebrated contributor. For this second success in his writing career had not lessened Nimrod's conceit and it was about this time that he addressed the following letter to his editor:

My name in the market is now good and I do not arrogate too much when I assert that the time is approaching when it will be better. This assertion may surprise you; fame, you will say, should be the consequence, not the motive of our actions, and we should not proclaim ourselves to the world. But I will not use the fulsome language of mock humility! A consciousness of merit is inseparable from the possession of it; and I should barely dissemble if I did not fearlessly declare, that on sporting subjects my pen shall yield to none other.[4]

He was quite accurate in what he said but he could perhaps have phrased it more modestly.

Surtees had to find ways round the embargo on the use of Nimrod's name whilst at the same time capitalizing on his fame and popularity. To that end he hit upon the ingenious ideas of instituting a series to be called 'Noctes Nimrodianae' or 'Sporting Conversations with Nimrod'. These purported to be written by the editor, Surtees, from discussions about hunting and sport generally which he had had with Nimrod and so, to use Surtees's own words, 'it could hardly be said they came within the scope of the bond prohibiting Nimrod from *writing* on sporting'. The idea was borrowed from *Blackwood's* 'Noctes Ambrosianae', a series of imaginary conversations contributed by Wilson, Hogg, Lockhart, and Maginn. The articles in the *New Sporting* were all, of course, written by Nimrod himself. Surtees was sailing just about as close to the wind as he possibly could but he was in luck, for no action followed. Although Surtees subsequently criticized the articles as 'pale imitations' of their progenitor, he had to admit that they 'caught on' and considerably increased the popularity of the magazine.

By now Nimrod was proving his worth to the magazine over and over again. In 1832 Surtees, swallowing whatever personal distaste he may have felt for his star contributor, crossed to Calais to interview him. Until that time they had not met, and Surtees must have seemed very small beer to Nimrod. He was merely an editor who had not published anything beyond a legal textbook and whose articles did not bear his real name.

Surtees's report of the visit and the subsequent character sketch he wrote of Nimrod display none of the venom with which he was subsequently to harry the older man right up to his death and, indeed, after it. The two articles, in fact, stand almost as exercises in sycophancy, a trait Surtees despised above all others. Whether Surtees was writing what he knew his readers wanted to hear, or whether he had been temporarily won over by Nimrod's undoubted charm, the result was temperate and generous: 'In appearance', he wrote of that first meeting,

he is tall and well-proportioned with a keen, penetrating eye, and very broad expanse of forehead. The society in which he has moved all his life is a sufficient guarantee for the politeness of his manner while the experience of life in all its varieties, with a naturally quick conception, and highly cultivated mind render him one of the most agreeable companions it is possible to conceive . . .

And in the portrait which followed a little later:

As a classical scholar, too, he stands high, paradoxical as such an accomplishment may appear in the eyes of those who judge of sportsmen in the description given of them by Fielding and writers of the last century . . . *It has ever been our practice to speak of people as we find them* [author's italics] and we feel a pleasure in stating that, in all our dealings and transactions, we have ever found him activated by the strictest sense of honour and the truest spirit of liberality. . . . He will be free at the end of next year, when he will come back like a 'giant refreshed' and attend the funeral of our old contemporary, who, we are happy to assure our readers, we are beating in a canter.[5]

Surtees's confidence in Nimrod's abilities on his return was not misplaced. Once he resumed writing under his own name he produced for the *New Sporting* two series of articles, 'Hunting Reminiscences' and 'The Crack Riders of England' which earned the comment from his editor that they were the best thing he had done for the magazine and contained much of his old fire. He was not idle in other quarters either for he produced for the *Quarterly* a successor to 'The Chace' called 'The Road' which was written from his knowledge of coaches and coachmen and from his own experiences on the box. It was every bit as successful as its predecessor. Lockhart, quite carried away, declared he 'could hunt like Hugo Meynell and write like Walter Scott', and even Surtees could find, then or later, nothing in it to criticize.

But when the third article, 'The Turf', for which Lockhart and Murray paid one hundred guineas (a very large sum in those days), appeared in the *Quarterly* to make up a trilogy Surtees had grave reservations as to its accuracy and authority. Since he was still in the process of 'buttering up' his famous contributor he kept these reservations to himself until after Nimrod's death when he expressed them brutally and in his own savage fashion, quoting as his justification a conversation in the 'Noctes Nimrodianae' where Nimrod had incautiously allowed the following remark of his to be published: 'Why, you are not perhaps aware that no man knows or cares less about racing than I do, and every year that passes over my head makes me care less.'

Nimrod in fact knew a great deal about racing. He had both trained and ridden with success himself and was regarded as an authority on the interpretation of the rules. What prompted the remark it is impossible now to ascertain but his biographer says, almost certainly accurately, that he intended it to mean that he did not care for racing unless he was actively concerned with it and at that time, living in Calais, of course he was not. Whatever prompted the remark Surtees seized on it as a peg upon which to hang his attack on 'The Turf'. 'Now Nimrod,' he wrote 'of all people under the sun was the least qualified for the task, for he had not the slightest taste or inclination for racing, added to which his acquaintance was chiefly amongst hunting men and he had nobody to go to for information . . . He had to read up his subject and of course wrote with the fear and trepidation of a man who attempts to enlighten others on a subject he does not himself understand . . .'[6] The comment was as inaccurate as it was uncalled for and he found few to agree with him. 'This fellow dips his pen in magic!' was the verdict of one well-known racing authority on reading the article, 'for I can hear the horses breathe, and the silk jackets rustle as they go by me.'[7] Surtees either had not bothered to check his facts—a fault he was always prone to—or else, much more likely, was allowing personal prejudices to blind him to them.

All his writing life, whether as editor or author, Surtees never appreciated the power of the printed word to hurt. Once he had secured Nimrod's services he summarily disposed of those of Dashwood. He disliked Dashwood and Dashwood was, it is true, a poor, prosy writer. Nevertheless, having rid himself of him, one might have expected he would have allowed him to disappear in peace into the obscurity he felt he merited. But not at all. Surtees continued constantly to pillory him in print, referring to him always as 'a noodle', or 'Donkey

Dashwood pricking his long ears' at some piece of information, worthless or otherwise. It is the case that writers were less restrained in their comments then than now and the law of libel was less stringently interpreted and applied, but even so much of what Surtees wrote went perilously close to the borders of fair comment and on occasions crossed them. Before long this got him, or rather Ackermann as the printer and publisher of the magazine, into trouble.

Surtees had been staying with his friend Herbert Langham at Cottesbroke Park in Northamptonshire. They had a few days with Squire Osbaldeston who was then hunting the Pytchley. For a change and, no doubt, on Surtees's part, with the intention of gathering fresh copy, they decided to pay a visit to the Warwickshire. To do this they had to send their horses on and to put themselves up at Leamington.

Surtees had already had experience of the two principal hotels in Leamington, the Regent and the Royal. Both, he said, were inferior and uncomfortable so they booked into the Bedford, then kept by a Mr Gomm. This, as they discovered to their sorrow, was a mistake. 'I have a perfect recollection now', Surtees wrote long afterwards, 'of a great, raw-looking lump of carrion that used to mount guard on the dusty sideboard every morning, enough to give one a fit of indigestion for the rest of the day.'[8] Fortunately for him and Mr Ackermann he did not print this in his subsequent article, but what he did say was sufficient to make Mr Gomm consult his lawyers and, as a result, a writ for libel was issued:

As for the Bedford *by Gumm* no one should think of going there who has not a hardy constitution and a long purse; and the large hotels are too numerous and too empty to spare many guests for the small ones. Still we can hardly say we are sorry for the innkeepers, for there certainly never were a more rapacious set gathered together, as every person that has ever had any dealings with them can testify . . .

This was no worse than many of Surtees's other tart comments but on this occasion he met someone who was determined to preserve his reputation and pursue his remedy.

Surtees, of course, would neither withdraw a word, nor settle or compromise in any way. He briefed a Mr Davenport Hill, MP, a leading counsel, to conduct his defence. Hill advised that their only chance was to try to laugh the case out of court. This, as every lawyer knows and Surtees himself as a lawyer must have known, is one of the most difficult courses any advocate can adopt and is usually only taken as a last resort. If it goes wrong the results are disastrous and the damages enormous. Surtees, always ready for a fight, was prepared to accept the risk and instructed Hill to take the line he advised.

Gomm's original claim was for £500 damages but he applied to amend this by increasing it to £1,000. The judge before whom the application came permitted the amendment indicating that he took a serious view of the libel.

But when the case was heard before the Lord Chief Justice and a special jury Mr Hill scored a resounding success. He made a fool of the unfortunate Gomm in the box and in a witty closing speech had the jury fully with him and laughing at his sallies. Surtees says that the Lord Chief at times joined in the laughter, but in the event he summed up against him. The jury, however, were for once more influenced by counsel than the judge and they brought in the contemptuous verdict of a farthing damages.

Surtees had been very lucky but he himself did not think so. He thought the lawyers a pack of fools or knaves to advise Gomm to bring his action and the Lord Chief one or the other for summing up against him. It did not persuade him to moderate either his views or his language nor did it decrease his dislike and contempt for the law and its practitioners.

To add to his other preoccupations during all this time, because of the failing health of both his parents Surtees was much at Hamsterley, helping to run the estate. Where he had once derided railways he now had reason to be thankful for them since, although most of the journey to Durham had still to be made by coach, there were local lines springing up to help him on his way. 'Who would abolish railways?' he wrote. 'They are the great civilisers of our time.' And, elaborating on the same subject a little later: 'In the last century there was only one coach between Edinburgh and London which was from twelve to sixteen days on the road. Before another year elapses, the journey between the two capitals will be done in one day.'

Even with the help of the railway only a man of his immense drive, energy, and physical resources could have got through the work he did, dealing at Hamsterley with tenants' wants and complaints, helping his father to supervise the extensive home farm and, in London, editing, writing, coping with contributors, as well as making his extensive hunting tours and expeditions.

He was at Hamsterley when Nimrod visited there on his 'Northern Tour', the last hunting tour in England he was able to undertake. He did so at the invitation of Lord Kintore who, along with other leading sportsmen in Scotland and in the north, mounted him on the best for his last fling across the hunting countries. Once again he resumed his semi-regal progress and was entertained at all the best houses and finest mansions. The pick of their owners' studs were put at his disposal and, although now approaching sixty, he showed that he had lost nothing of his old dash when crossing a country. So impressed was the Duke of Buccleuch that he ordered a horse to be at the covert-side for him every day he wished to come out with the Buccleuch Hounds. Nimrod revelled in it all as a welcome return to the years of his glory. Nor did it in any way lessen his self-esteem.

When he came to Hamsterley, 'Mr Surtees junior' as he referred to his editor in his subsequent report, met him at Newcastle with the Surtees carriage. The account of the visit, when published, ignored Surtees altogether and concentrated on his father:

A true sample of the old English Squire and as good a judge of a horse, a hound, a bottle of port wine, and an oak-tree, as any man in England, or anywhere else . . . Previously to my setting out for the North, a report had reached me that Mr Surtees was unwell . . . but I am happy to say that, although he may feel something of the *non sum qualis eram* about himself, from the knocks and bumps to which we foxhunters are subject—in addition to having seen nearly half a score of Christmas days since then—I saw not the slightest alteration in either his appearance or his spirits. I can only say that, following the example set me by my host, and by the help of sundry other irresistible allurements, I drank more claret during the five or six days I spent at Hamsterley than I had done in the space of time for many a long day before.[9]

Nimrod may, of course, have been complying with Surtees's expressed desire for anonymity and dislike of publicity in avoiding any direct reference to him but it seems strange all the same that no mention at all of 'Surtees junior' appears in his account. The practical joke which Surtees played on him may however have had something to do with this and certainly cannot have inspired him with any desire to effuse in print on the virtues of his host's son.

Always anxious to do what he could to puncture Nimrod's vanity, Surtees brought him out hunting with Sir Matthew White-Ridley's Hounds. To his great delight he found that no member of the field recognized his guest as the famous hunting correspondent, Nimrod. Immediately he decided to conceal the stranger's real identity and he introduced him as a London visitor having his first day with hounds and who therefore required help and instruction. Mr Morby, a tailor who came out regularly, volunteered to look after the supposed tyro and, according to Surtees, 'gave him some very accurate information about hunting'. He also pointed out a moth-hole in Nimrod's breeches and recommended a way of repairing it. So delighted was Surtees with the success of his ruse that he chuckled over it for the rest of his days.

Though he could not at that moment have known it, Surtees had every reason to show more kindliness and respect towards Nimrod than he did, for, as it happened, one of the most successful serials ever to appear in the *New Sporting* was beginning to run contemporaneously with Nimrod's 'Northern Tour', and it came from the same hand.

Three years previously, while he was still living in Calais, Nimrod had heard a tremendous knocking at his front door. Opening it himself without waiting for his servant he found his old friend, Squire Mytton of Halston, standing on the threshold. But it was not the magnificent figure of the 'Mad Jack' Mytton he remembered well. Gone was the great frame which had carried Mytton through a hundred escapades. It had enabled him to shoot duck from a frozen lake clad only in his night-shirt on the coldest of winter nights without suffering the slightest chill, and to force his horse at the end of a long hunt over five feet of iron park-railings to be in at the kill, evoking from the Master the admiring cry: 'Well done, neck or nothing. You are not a bad one to breed from!' But now Nimrod saw 'a round-shouldered, decrepit, tottering *old young* man, if I may be allowed such a term, and so bloated by drink that I might have exclaimed with Ovid, Accedant capiti cornua *Bacchus eris*'. (If you had but horns on your head you would be Bacchus.)

'In God's name,' Nimrod exclaimed. 'What brought you to France?'

'Just what brought yourself,' was his friend's reply with a flash of his old fire. 'Three couple of bailiffs were hard at my brush.'[10]

As we know Nimrod took Mytton in, looked after him, and found him comfortable lodgings. Under his care and supervision Mytton might have revived and survived but even in his present condition the quiet life was not for him. He soon returned to England and died three years later in a debtor's prison.

Nimrod had always been fascinated by Mytton and the paradoxes and contradictions presented by his character. In his sober moments Mytton was quiet and cultivated, a man of charm and distinction. The contrast between his wild exploits—dressing up as a highwayman and holding up his guests after a dinner party, riding a bear into a dining-room during another, scattering thousands of pounds in bank notes representing his winnings at Doncaster from his carriage window on the way home, exclaiming 'light come, light go', setting the leader of his gig at a turnpike gate to find out from the dealer who sat beside him 'if he was a good timber jumper',—and the quiet, thoughtful, kind-hearted man buried deep within him whom Nimrod was one of the few to know, made him determined to write his life. Nimrod initially put the project to Surtees who was dismissive of Mytton as a mere debauchee and he turned it down. Nimrod, however, was not to be deterred, and without waiting for a commission he sat down and wrote the life. When it was completed he sent it to Lockhart hoping that he would accept it for the *Quarterly*. While appreciating its qualities and saying so, Lockhart did not think it suitable for his serious magazine so Nimrod turned once more to Surtees and the *New Sporting*. Having read the manuscript Surtees was still doubtful about its chances of success. However, he knew the pulling power of Nimrod's name and so he consulted with Ackermann who also read it. 'With some serious misgivings' they decided to publish it as a serial. To their astonishment it proved so popular that they had to double their print order to cope with the demand. It was later published by Ackermann in book form with illustrations by Henry Alken. The first edition sold out immediately; a second, larger one, proved equally popular and also sold well, extraordinarily enough, in America. Despite its unlikely subject it is a spirited, lively, and literate memoir of a life so exaggeratedly misspent as to generate its own attraction, and it has been reprinted many times since.

The serial materially helped the sales and reputation of the *New Sporting* so that Surtees's later sour comment that 'We do not think the work calculated to raise the literary reputation of Nimrod. It is a sad jumble of inconsistencies, of accusation and palliation, keeping the reader in a state of suspense as to which side the author really means to espouse, and generally, we should think, leaving him with the impression that it is a work that would have been much better let alone', seems both unkind and uncalled for. His opinion may, however, have been coloured by the fact that the second edition of *Jaunts and*

Jollities was published by Ackermann at about the same time and proved a resounding failure.

It was Nimrod, too, who, generous and magnanimous as ever, brought Jorrocks to the notice of Lockhart. Nimrod's friendship with both Murray and Lockhart had grown since the success of his initial articles. Even the arrogant and aloof Lockhart seems to have fallen under the spell of his charm and Murray certainly did, for he made a point of entertaining him to literary dinners whenever Nimrod was in London. It was at one of these dinners that Nimrod mentioned Jorrocks to Lockhart. At this time as well as featuring him in the 'Jaunts and Jollities' series in the *New Sporting* Surtees was using the grocer as a sort of filler-in and prop and stay to the magazine, producing from him comments in uninhibited cockney on all manner of sporting matters and publishing open letters over his name, also couched in cockney, directed to or against those who had offended him or who had broken what he considered to be the true canons of fox-hunting or other behaviour. 'The most useful man to the work [i.e. the magazine]', Surtees wrote long afterwards, 'beyond all question, though I say it who perhaps should not, was Mr Jorrocks, the sporting grocer of Great Coram Street, who not only followed all field sports, but indulged in diverse vagaries not connected therewith. Jorrocks could turn his hand to almost anything.'[11]

Extraordinarily enough for one of his sedentary and fastidious tastes (though perhaps it is an explanation of his excellence as an editor), Lockhart appears to have been fascinated by the idea of Jorrocks, the cockney, holding himself up as an authority on all things connected with the aristocratic and exclusive pursuit of the fox and other esoteric sporting matters. Acting on Nimrod's recommendation, as Surtees himself admits, he wrote to Surtees as follows: 'I believe you are the creator of Jorrocks who has always delighted me. Do get some cousin of his in the horsey line, and throw the materials into light dramatic form . . .' (The rest of the letter is missing.)[12]

It is believed that it was this endorsement from such an

august and unlikely quarter that gave Surtees the necessary encouragement to write a serial with John Jorrocks as the chief character, a serial which would expound through the mouth of Jorrocks all Surtees's thoughts on hunting, his hopes and fears for the sport, his prejudices against many who took part in it and his praises for the few, the very few, who came up to his exacting standards for its true, correct, and traditional conduct. It was this serial which, after many vicissitudes, was eventually published in book form as *Handley Cross* and Nimrod, paradoxically enough, the most traduced character in it, may well have claims to have sowed the seed which inspired it.

Surtees's spell as an editor was beginning to draw to a close. He was under considerable pressure from his other obligations and interests and much of his writing thoughts, too, must now have been turning towards the further and fuller adventures of John Jorrocks, who was to be given new-found dignity as an MFH. In the previous year, 1835, Surtees had removed his name from the law list and given up forever any tenuous connection he might have maintained with the law and its practice. It has been said that this was the result of his having agreed to enter into a solicitor's partnership with an individual who has remained unnamed, and that this individual attempted to defraud him of the money he had advanced to set up the joint practice. This statement, which has been dignified by appearing in the *Dictionary of National Biography,* is almost certainly incorrect. No record of any such transaction exists either in the Law Society or elsewhere, nor does any reference to it occur in the fragmentary memoirs which Surtees left behind him. Had it happened Surtees would almost certainly have either recorded it or used it somewhere in his fiction. No such traumatic occurrence would have been overlooked by him with his retentive memory and ability to transmute all experience into expression on the printed page. Mr Cuming, his first biographer and the discoverer of his archives, rightly dismisses it as a fable and suggests that it came from an unfounded assertion in an unsigned memoir to a later edition of the *Jaunts and Jollities*. Surtees, as we know, had no liking for the law. He was now well established in journalism, he had Hamsterley to look after, and it was above all unlikely that he would have contemplated a partnership in a profession whose ethics he scorned and whose practice he despised, especially at a time when other pressures were bearing hard upon him.

As might have been expected with one of his temperament these pressures made him ever more touchy and difficult to deal with. He had a serious quarrel with a man called J. W. Carleton who wrote as 'Craven' for several magazines, sporting and otherwise, which was to have repercussions, and relations with Ackermann, too, were deteriorating. The exact causes of the coolness between Ackermann and himself are unknown but it seems clear that for reasons of his own which may have been connected with the ever-present risk of libel when Surtees was given a free hand, and from which they had so recently had such a lucky escape, Ackermann was anxious to dispose of his interest in the magazine. Negotiations were set on foot to value their respective shares and to find a buyer. It may have been hoped that Harrison Ainsworth, another lawyer who had exchanged 'certainty for a chance' by abandoning his senior partnership in a family firm* to devote all his time to writing, would come forward as a buyer. Ainsworth was a close friend of Thackeray's, he was a horseman himself 'and had just enjoyed an enormous success with *Rookwood*, a highly romanticized story of Dick Turpin and his ride to York, for which he had travelled on horseback himself from London to York 'to verify distances and localities'. Ainsworth was known to have ambitions as an editor. Subsequently he bought and sold several magazines, in one of which he was responsible for the initial success of *Mr Sponge's Sporting Tour*. But at that time he was not, apparently, ready to take the plunge into publishing and proprietorship

---

* 'A youth foredoom'd his father's hopes to cross, who penned a stanza when he should engross.'

and he was, besides, enjoying enormously the social success which the sales and popularity of *Rookwood* had brought him. He did not then come forward but he had by no means passed out of Surtees's life.

Matters were brought to a head when, in November 1836, Surtees received an invitation to stand for Gateshead as a Parliamentary Conservative candidate in the coming election. This request, if it was accepted, would render it all but impossible for him to continue to edit a sporting magazine in London. He was complimented by the approach, anxious to do what he could for the electors of the county, and disposed to allow his name to go forward. Since no offers to purchase the magazine had as yet been made, he decided to advertise it for sale. The following advertisement, which bears every indication of being drafted by Surtees's own hand, appeared in its next issue:

The 'New Sporting Magazine' was established by gentlemen who carried it on more for amusement than profit, consequently it has not attained the circulation it is capable of. It has, however, been steadily increasing without the aid of advertising, and the gross receipts are now about £2,000 a year; and it will be sold at such a price as will yield a very large profit on the present circulation.[13]

It has been said that no buyer appeared in response to this advertisement but this again is incorrect. In fact a Mr Spiers, 'a talented and deserving tradesman' according to Surtees, who had all along printed the magazine, bought out Ackermann's controlling interest and became both proprietor and publisher, while Surtees retained his own minority share. Very honourably in view of his other commitments and the fact that he was damaging his prospects of election to Parliament by being unable adequately to canvas the constituency, he agreed to continue as editor until the New Year in order to give Spiers time to secure an adequate replacement. Then, having penned a gracious farewell message to his readers, contributors, literary friends and supporters, he put aside his editor's pen forever and returned to

Durham. He was succeeded in the editorial chair by George Tattersall who wrote and drew under the pen-name of 'Wildrake'.

On 6 January 1837, almost immediately after his return from London, Surtees's mother died. His father, also in ill health, was grief-stricken at his loss. The entire responsibility for running the estate and controlling the colliery interests which have never been explicitly defined but which must have made a considerable contribution to the family income, now fell upon Surtees's shoulders. In addition, he had also the burden of his Parliamentary candidature.

It was an exceedingly complicated state of affairs which brought Surtees into politics for the first and last time and which made the Conservative interest so anxious for him to stand. Mr Rippon, a Liberal, was the sitting member. He was not popular for he was believed to exploit his position for his own ends rather than those of his constituents and, moreover, his private life did not stand up to scrutiny. He was being opposed by a Mr Williamson, a much more worthy character, but one who would also stand as a Liberal. It was, however, thought that Mr Williamson would attract much of the Conservative vote in order to get Rippon out. This did not commend itself to the Conservative organization and, seeing the possibility of a split Liberal vote if they could put forward a convincing candidate themselves, they thought they might well win the seat. From this sprang the approach to Surtees and his acceptance. He had already dashed off an address to the electors before his return to Hamsterley in the New Year but now, owing to the death of his mother, it was not proper, he thought, to resume active campaigning until a decent interval had elapsed. Though he did what he could during this time and his supporters were, of course, active, Mr Williamson was able to make capital out of his inaction and attracted the promises of a considerable number of Conservative votes. The fight, therefore, became a three-cornered one with the issues clouded on all sides. In an effort to resolve them before things had gone too far Surtees made an offer to Mr Williamson:

Several gentlemen have promised you their votes under the impression that no other candidate of their Conservative opinions would offer himself, and they will remain true to their promises in spite of their politics. My remaining in the field therefore, will only have the effect of producing uncertainty, and of returning Mr Rippon should we go to a poll. I will at once then withdraw my address if you will agree, in the event of Mr R's retiring, to release all your promises, and let us have a *friendly* struggle on political principles...I should observe that in coming forward I was actuated by no unfriendly feeling towards yourself. The information I received in the south induced me to believe that you were coming forward more to oblige the electors than from any desire of obtaining the seat; and wishing to see the representation of the borough kept among the gentry of the district, I was induced to place myself in competition...[14]

This proposition, not unnaturally, commended itself neither to Mr Williamson nor Mr Rippon, who both continued to stand and fight. Accordingly Surtees set about drawing up a fuller and more comprehensive address to the electors on his own behalf. As might have been expected this address when finally finished and despatched was manly, straightforward, and uncompromising. A conservative both by nature and conviction as a landowner and farmer, in both those interests he was a protectionist; as a member of the gentry by birth and breeding he was no believer in the equality of man despite the savaging in his books later on of those at the top of the social scale who abused privilege and exercised power unbridled and unchecked. He would not, therefore, support any extension of the franchise and said so in the clearest of terms. As an honest document setting out fairly and squarely the attitudes of a reasonable Conservative of his time the address has interest today:

I am a decided Friend to Improvement in every Shape—and Way—a Reformer of Proved Abuses in Church and State—an

Advocate for the fullest Measure of Civil and Religious Liberty that is compatible with the Security of Property and the Maintenance of a National Religion—for Retrenchment and Economy in every Department of the Public Service—for the Extension of Commerce, the Reduction of Taxation, particularly of those that press heavily on the Working Population, for the Difusion of Useful Knowledge throughout the Country...The Franchise I consider sufficiently low, to place it within the Reach of all Men of Prudence and Industry, to whom its attainment is an Object of Ambition...[15]

Although the address was well received and won many friends both Liberal and Conservative, it came too late to have great impact and Mr Williamson, while evading any direct confrontation with Surtees, continued his campaign to ensure that the promises of support made by his Conservative friends would be kept at the polls and, of course, one vote in those days meant far more than it does today. While the radical press took the opportunity of attacking Surtees's policies in the most violent terms, neither they nor anyone else had a word to say against the man himself. 'The bold and frank demeanour of Mr Surtees deserved radical approbation, and made that gentleman an object of respectful treatment...' was only one of the many compliments paid to him.

At that time voting was by a show of hands unless a poll was required, and after the count Mr Rippon was declared elected. However someone, presumably Mr Williamson or his agent, then required a poll to be taken. Believing that his own and Mr Williamson's vote was hopelessly split Surtees decided to withdraw. From a purely political point of view this was a mistake, for Williamson was not only a weak candidate who had avoided taking a stance on any of the issues of the campaign, but had also allowed himself to fall between the Liberal and Conservative stools. At 3.15 p.m. on the day of the poll Rippon had secured 236 votes to Williamson's 151, and Williamson accordingly conceded defeat.

Had he persisted, Surtees, in view of his personal standing and the admiration he had engendered for the manner in which he had conducted his campaign, might well have secured a surprise victory over two weak and undeserving candidates. His motives in withdrawing, as usual with him, appear to have been mixed. Ostensibly it was his wish not to split the opposition vote, and this unquestionably played a part in his decision but not, it may be suggested, the whole part. He might just have won but it would have been in the words of the great man of whose horsemanship he had been so unjustly critical, 'a damned close-run thing.'

Surtees was never averse to a fight but he always wanted to be sure of winning, or at least to be able to assure himself in the many controversies in which he engaged that he had emerged the winner. Victory at the polls was by no means certain. A withdrawal with dignity was far more fitting than the humiliation of defeat by either of his opponents, both of whose characters had been assaulted in the Press, Williamson for his pusillanimity in not facing Surtees and declaring himself, Rippon for his private life and doubtful probity. Surtees certainly spoke the truth when he told Williamson he had had to be persuaded to take up the task. His heart was not in it. He was a countryman, a sportsman, and a writer. His forceful, outspoken character would have driven him to detest the tedium of debate, the falseness, deviousness, and fickleness of Parliamentary ways and means even more than he had loathed the whole ethic and practice of the law. This is borne out by the fact that his demeanour and campaign having so impressed observers, he was constantly not only asked but implored to allow his name to go forward again and was adamant in his refusals. He even turned down a personal request to stand for the City of Durham from Lord Londonderry, one of the greatest and most influential of the northern noblemen.

It must have increased his distaste for the whole business of politics that before the winter was out he was asked to act as second in a challenge arising out of the election. An old friend of his, John Hodgson Hinde, was the sitting member for Newcastle. A quarrel arose between him and a Major Orde over some action Orde had taken in disputing the fairness of

John Leech.
Watercolour by John
Everett Millais, 1854

Mark Lemon

William Makepeace
Thackeray. Portrait
by Samuel Lawrence,
c. 1864

Letter from Thackeray to
Surtees acknowledging
numbers of *Mr Sponge's
Sporting Tour,* 1849

Sir   This is not to thank you for
the Grouse; but for the 2 last
numbers of *Soapey Sponge,* they are
capital, the Flat Hats delightful:
those fellows in spectacles divine: &
Scamperdale's character perfectly
odious & admirable. I am come
down hither in search of strength &
fresh air.
      Ever yours truly dear Surtees
W. M. Thackeray

If I've forgot your Xtian name don't
quarrel with me

Hinde's brother Richard's election to a seat at Berwick. A Colonel Younghusband was acting for Orde and Hinde asked Surtees to stand for him. Apparently Hinde had little fear of the outcome for in his letter to Surtees setting out the facts of the case, he added the laconic comment 'Dull fighting weather this, and injurious to hair-triggers'.

Younghusband, too, thought the matter a trivial one, as indeed it appeared to be. Surtees, who, as he was later to show on the Bench, was level-headed enough when it came to quarrels other than his own, agreed with him and together they managed between themselves to settle the matter peaceably and without bloodshed.

As it turned out it could not have been more fortunate for Surtees that he failed to find a seat in the election, for the year 1838 was to be a crowded and eventful one for him. On 8 March his father, worn out by grief and ill health, died very suddenly. Surtees thereupon succeeded him as the squire of Hamsterley and the inheritor of the family fortunes and obligations. Then Ralph Lambton, Surtees's idol and mentor, had the third of his terrible and crippling falls out hunting, as a result of which he was paralysed and confined to bed for the rest of his life. With no prospect of his ever hunting again he gave up the country and his pack was sold. This in turn meant that all the country round Hamsterley became vacant and unhunted. Surtees decided to form his own pack and hunt it himself, making only the terse entry in his diary, 'I got hounds', to mark the event.

Although his hunting experience from his tours and expeditions was as extensive as any man's, this was his first opportunity actually to hunt hounds since his ill-fated and comical venture with Colonel Charrittie at Boulogne. And, as he was shortly to put into the mouth of his alter ego, Mr Jorrocks, 'none but an 'untsman knows an 'untsman's cares'. But he entered into his new duties with a lively anticipation of pleasure in performing them. Had he been elected to Parliament he could scarcely have taken hounds and unquestionably the letters MFH meant far more to him than those of

MP: '"Talk of a MP! Vot's an MP compared to an MFH?" said Jorrocks J'.

Then, in the midst of all this, there seemed every likelihood of his having to fight a duel himself. Touchy as always he took the greatest offence at a reference made to him in an article by 'Craven' (J. W. Carleton). Ordinarily he would instantly have issued a challenge, but now that he was the squire of Hamsterley and an MFH he was concerned about the social niceties of the situation. Was it consistent with his new-found dignities and the *code duello* to call out a man now so far beneath him as a mere scribbler? In his dilemma he sought the assistance of his old friend, counsellor, and contributor, the painter, now Sir Francis Grant, who was on visiting terms with all the best people and upon whose advice he could rely.

Grant's reply merits reproducing in full since it demonstrates how persistent, despite its proscription by law, was the survival of duelling as a method of avenging insults and resolving personal quarrels. It illustrates, too, the rigid social code that dictated whom it was proper, according to one's station in life, to face 'with the saw-handles', as Surtees's Irish contemporary Charles Lever put it, and whom it was obligatory to ignore as beneath recognition.

RANTON ABBEY, STAFFS.

MY DEAR SURTEES,—It would never do for a Master of Foxhounds to fight an anonymous scribe* in the old Magazine. It would be *infra dig*.... Last night I was speaking with Lord Lichfield, with whom I am staying, about your case. He first said, not knowing your antagonist, that it is always safest to fight. He then said 'Do you know who is the man?' I said he signed himself Craven. 'Oh,' said he, 'that was the fellow whom Charles Greville had the row with the other day at Newmarket'; but Greville never for a moment thought of fighting him, which, if he had considered him as a gentleman, he would, of course, have done, as the language used and I believe, written, was most abusive. Lord Lichfield went on to say that he was

---

* It was only a matter of eighteen months or so since Surtees had been an 'anonymous scribe' himself!

one (I think I recollect right) of a Committee of the Jockey Club which sat in judgment on the case—not as to whether the gentlemen should fight, for that, of course, never entered into anybody's head—but whether or no the club should turn him off Newmarket Green, and prevent his ever appearing there again, a thing which it appears they have the right to do.

It strikes me this sets your question at rest. If Greville never could for a moment think of fighting him, I don't see how you can—unless it is an amusement which you particularly fancy.[16]

That, for the moment, ended what Mr Cuming calls Surtees's 'bloodthirsty intention' but, as was his way, he did not forget or forgive Carleton.

In addition to all these events the year 1838 saw the publication by Mr Spiers, the printer and proprietor of the *New Sporting,* of *Jorrocks's Jaunts and Jollities* in book form, with twelve uncoloured illustrations by Hablot K. Browne, who signed himself 'Phiz' and who was later to rise to fame as the illustrator of Charles Dickens's novels. Ackermann, who was far more experienced in handling sporting subjects than Spiers, was not offered the book. During the course of the year the already strained relations between Ackermann and Surtees had worsened, for it had come to Surtees's ears that Ackermann was backing the publication of yet another sporting magazine to be called the *Sporting Review,* and had installed as editor none other than the hated 'Craven'.

Most important of all, however, there appeared between March and June in the *New Sporting* a new series entitled 'The Gin and Water Hunt'. In this Surtees elevated John Jorrocks to the position of MFH and began to relate his exploits and adventures in that position. Uproarious, outrageous, and hugely comic, they were to give Surtees his place in English literature and to make his subject the most famous and most quoted Master of Foxhounds of all time.

CHAPTER SIX

Jorrocks

IT has been said with some truth that more people quote Jorrocks than read *Handley Cross*. Indeed in that sentence lies much of the explanation for the initial failure and subsequent success of Surtees's most famous book. John Jorrocks *is Handley Cross,* so much so that the book is often referred to by his name alone. Without him—and, as will be seen, he very nearly disappeared from its pages—the book would have remained in obscurity and been long forgotten. It has been called 'a blundering masterpiece' but in fact, considered as a whole, it is very far from being any sort of masterpiece. But its chief character is truly a masterpiece, for John Jorrocks stands assured of a place in the pantheon of great comic figures in English literature. He has been compared to Falstaff but he needs no such comparison, for he is a unique creation. So truly original is he that he has spawned no imitators although he is said to have given Dickens the inspiration for Pickwick.

When Henry Colburn first published *Handley Cross* he had doubts about his wisdom in handling it at all, and his doubts about his ability to sell it were speedily confirmed. In three volumes without illustrations it proved an almost total failure. A few years earlier Henry Colburn had given qualified encouragement to Nimrod when he was considering trying his hand at a sporting book, before he became famous as a sporting journalist. He was a shrewd, tough, opportunist publisher and a good judge of the market, who published Frances Trollope and who also brought out two of Anthony's early novels.

The early chapters of the serial give every impression of having been hurriedly dashed off by Surtees to meet a deadline or to fill in space. The serial changed its name in

June 1838 from 'The Gin and Water Hunt' to 'The Handley
Cross Hounds', and the further chapters appeared at irregular
intervals until August 1839 when the serial abruptly ended,
leaving the unfortunate Jorrocks confined as a lunatic on the
petition of his wife and relations, confirmed by the evidence of
the two doctors from Handley Cross, and also that of
Pomponius Ego, the thinly-disguised Nimrod. Pilloried in the
box by Jorrocks's counsel, Nimrod was given a hard time of it
in this concluding chapter and was held up to ridicule in the
most blatant and unsubtle fashion. More importantly, however, the scathing 'Pomponius Ego' pseudonym for Nimrod
and the 'ar niver gets off' incident which so seriously libelled
him in the book do not appear at all in the magazine.

During the year Surtees had been nursing yet another
grievance against Nimrod, feeling himself to have been not
only offended but badly treated by the older man, and for
once with some justification.

In the summer of 1838 it came to Spiers's notice that
Nimrod was flirting with the management of Ackermann's
new magazine in the hope of becoming its editor. When this
fell through he was being tempted by offers from the new
editor to transfer his allegiance from the *New Sporting* to the
Sporting Review. Spiers conveyed this piece of literary gossip to
Surtees who was enraged by it, and by the eventual
appointment of Carleton as editor. Carleton, it seemed, was
about to steal a march on him and acquire one of his best
authors. He does not appear to have paused to reflect that
Carleton was acting towards the *New Sporting* in exactly the
same way as he had done to his former employers when he
founded his own magazine. His wrath was increased when he
discovered that he was paying one of the penalties of
anonymity by reading in the New York *Spirit of the Times,* a
leading American magazine of 'the sporting literary and
fashionable world', the following sentences: 'In this department of literature Nimrod stands confessedly at the head of
English writers. He has recently brought to a close his famous
"Northern Tour" and is now engaged, as we suspect, upon

"Sporting Lectures" under the *nom de guerre* of "Jack Jorrocks"'. And he was further incensed to discover that Nimrod
had written a letter to Ackermann in which he said 'I think
the *New Sporting* is going wrong—so do many others'.

Nimrod, who had no contract with the *New Sporting,* was
perfectly entitled to take his work where he liked but he was
certainly injudicious when, in an implicit attempt to explain
his action, he wrote to *Bell's Life* complaining how the *New
Sporting* was rendering his work worthless by their innumer-
able ludicrous misprints in his recent contributions. *Bell's Life,*
delighted to stir up trouble, published his letter in full and in a
prominent place.

Spiers, on reading it, promptly wrote to Nimrod saying: 'I
was certainly surprised to see your letter in *Bell's Life in London,*
for I supposed I might have reasonably have expected that a
contributor to the *New Sporting Magazine,* if he did not
endeavour to advance that work, would, at least, refrain from
doing anything calculated to injure it; the concluding remarks
of which letter have evidently no other intention on the part of
the writer . . .'[1] A copy of this letter was sent by Spiers to Surtees
who found it far from strong enough. Although it was strictly
speaking not his quarrel, for he was no longer the editor of the
magazine, ever eager to strike a blow against Nimrod and to
enter into controversy with him or anyone else, he plunged into
the fray and a vitriolic correspondence ensued.

Nimrod, apparently touched on the raw by something that
had been said which he attributed—rightly—to Surtees, was
for once stirred out of his accustomed urbanity. He exploded
in print and into personalities, taking the opportunity,
unwisely perhaps in view of what was to happen, of
identifying his real enemy—Surtees—and doing so in the most
violent and abusive terms, so unlike his usual style as to show
how deeply he must have been hurt:

The malevolence of another party, who confessed in their pages that
I was 'the card they played for when they started their magazine,' is
now before you. Your readers, however, shall have a clue to the
author of this malevolent attack on me as a writer, and many of

them will, I think, recognize the portrait. He is a lanky north-countryman—the very antipodes of what his father was—long and weak, like the water-lizard, in his appearance, and partaking in his nature; and not a little either of another reptile, who is said to spit as well as crawl, but whose spit is, in my opinion, quite harmless, as the teeth of the viper proved when he attempted to bite the file...[2]

Surtees's reply was immediate. In the *New Sporting* he published at great length a refutation of Nimrod's original and subsequent complaints (despite the fact that he was no longer editor he appears to have been able to command unlimited space for his contributions, personal or otherwise), adding to it an open letter to Nimrod purporting to have been written by Jorrocks. It was couched in the silliest, abusive, and least convincing vein of Surtees's pseudo-cockney, but it gave him the opportunity not only to attack Nimrod once more publicly in print but also to have a side-swipe, as it were, at Carleton:

DEAR DADDY, [it began]
You're goin' it! I've just been a readin' of the *Life* as usual, and, upon my life, I couldn't have believed you'd have written sich a letter, only I know you'd got out of our coach again, and taken the situation of cad to Mr Craven. And talking of Mr Craven, dear dad, reminds me of a wery instructive letter I once had the pleasure of writing him respecting the wery matter I have to find fault with you about—bein too personal, or not sufficiently anonymous in your innuendoors... Wot I wants to give you is a bit of adwice—whole-some, rational and good—never indulge in personalities—there's nothin' so wulgar as callin of names—any blackguard can do that...[3]

The quarrel, and the published exchanges it engendered, has importance beyond its apparently trivial nature for it has a bearing on the difficulty in getting *Handley Cross* published, and it also marks the final rupture, so far as Surtees was concerned, between him and Nimrod. There can be no doubt that, whatever had gone before, thenceforward Surtees regarded Nimrod as a declared enemy, to be openly sneered at, derided, caricatured, and pilloried in print on every possible occasion.

While all this was going on Surtees was still at work on *Handley Cross,* expanding it and tidying it up for future publication. The Sportin' Lectors (which, for many, are the best parts of the book) had already appeared separately in the magazine and unassociated with the serial. Surtees spatch-cocked these into the text and saved Jorrocks from permanent incarceration in Hoxton Lunatic Asylum by the intervention of Charley Stobbs and Mr Bowker, culminating in the scene between Jorrocks and the Lord Chancellor where Jorrocks, unaware of whom he is addressing, convinces the great man of his sanity by offering him, amongst other sage advice: 'If ever you keep 'ounds, always 'ave a year's meal in advance. Old goes 'alf as far again as new'.

The work on *Handley Cross* was of necessity slow for Surtees was at the same time maintaining his interest in the *New Sporting,* keeping in touch with George Tattersall, the current editor, and contributing articles to it and to *Bell's Life.* In addition he was hunting hounds himself at his own expense two days a week. By 1840, however, he was having trouble with his country and his hounds. 'Scarcely anyone hunted with me,' he recorded, 'except such friends as happened to be staying with me.'[4] Since, as we know, he was 'no advocate for leapin'', this must have made things difficult for him for he would have had no one to give him a lead or make holes in the fences. In fact the nicest thing one of his guests could find to say of his ability to ride to his hounds was that he was 'a good but careful horseman, endued with an eye for country, and an instinctive knowledge of the way hounds would run. Whence, though no thruster, he rarely failed to see what they were doing'.[5] His expenses, too, were mounting, and then there was trouble with farmers. His hounds were accused of worrying sheep and the accusation was brought home. Immediately he had the whole pack put down and announced his intention of giving up the country. He then leased it to the Slaley Hunt, a neighbouring pack. More trouble followed and a hunting row developed for another pack, the Prudhoe and Derwent, disputed his right to grant the lease. They proceeded to draw his coverts and hunt over his land. This culminated in Surtees threatening an action for trespass against the Prudhoe and Derwent committee. The action never came on for the threat was sufficient to make the Prudhoe and Derwent withdraw. The hunt was subsequently disbanded and went out of existence and the country was successfully hunted by the Slaley Hounds for many years afterwards.

Then, too, during those years, Surtees was courting. On 19 May 1841 at Bishopswearmouth Parish Church he married Elizabeth Jane Fenwick, daughter of a neighbouring landowner and JP, Mr Addison Fenwick of Field House, Co. Durham, and Pallion Hall. It was an eminently suitable match. Two daughters and a son, christened Anthony as were all first sons born to the Surtees family, were the issue of the marriage.

Second sons who succeed unexpectedly are prone to take themselves and their positions more seriously than those who have them as of right by birth, and Surtees seems to have been no exception. Now that he was the squire, a tinge of self-importance lacking before appears both in himself, as exemplified by his conduct over the proposed duel with Carleton, and in his writings. Immediately, too, he began to play a full part in the county and its affairs for in 1842 he was appointed a JP and made Deputy Lieutenant for Durham.

He was an earnest, painstaking, and attentive magistrate who was just and fair in his decisions. He was courteous to all, save on occasions to certain lawyers whom, not without cause, he distrusted and disliked and whom later he was mercilessly to caricature in print. On the Bench his knowledge of law was of immense assistance to him and his fellow magistrates. He took detailed notes of all the cases upon which he sat, writing on thin blue paper and preserving the sheets for reference. They were a reservoir upon which he could draw not only for precedents in his judicial work but also for subsequent events and characters in his books. Some of Mr Jorrocks's experiences before and on the Bench in *Hillingdon Hall* are unquestionably based on them. He used the same blue paper for his manuscripts and his journalism. The notes were never destroyed and his scattered jottings for his proposed memoir together with certain important copies of correspondence lay intermingled with them for over half a century after his death until discovered by the hunting historian E. D. Cuming, proving a treasure trove indeed for his pioneer work on Surtees's life and experiences.

After his marriage, although he had given up hounds, Surtees continued to go on the hunting tours for which he had formed such a taste when editing the *New Sporting*. These tours were mostly round the northern countries and during them he no longer had to endure the discomforts of either inns or coaches, for he travelled either on the spreading railway network or by private carriage, and put up at the houses of friends. Here again the characters he met and the experiences he either enjoyed or suffered were stored away for future use in the books, serials, sketches, and articles which were shortly to pour from his pen.

In the summer, during the months of June and July, he and Mrs Surtees would journey to London and Brighton, some-times crossing to France to spend a few days in Paris. To reach London they travelled in their own coach to the railway terminus at Darlington forty miles away, over rough and hilly roads, the coach or 'chariot' as they called it, drawn by a team of four horses. On occasions they would have attached to the train a waggon or truck specially constructed for the purpose, on which they would place their coach and make the whole journey in their own private conveyance, the horses and servants being accommodated elsewhere on the train. This not only ensured privacy and increased comfort but also meant that they had their own carriage at their disposal on arrival at their destination. This method of travelling for well-to-do families was not at all unusual in the early days of rail.

During these visits to London Surtees improved his acquaintanceship with many of the literary men of the day, entertaining Lockhart, Ainsworth, Tom Hood, and a little later, W. M. Thackeray, dining with them in their clubs and houses in return. The friendship with Lockhart ripened and it was to Lockhart that he turned for advice on the construction and method of publishing *Handley Cross*. For, despite all the interruptions, work on the book was progressing well and it was beginning to take what he considered to be its final shape.

When he had it as he thought finished and ready for the press he sent the manuscript to Spiers for printing. In those days when typewriters did not exist printing often came before final arrangements for publication were made. As he received the proofs he sent them on, sheet by sheet, to Lockhart for his advice. At some period during this time Lockhart either wrote or remarked to Surtees, 'Apperley would rather be noticed than not', and Surtees appears to have taken this as justification for writing into the book the cruel caricature and satire on Nimrod and his work contained in the 'Pomponius Ego' chapters of *Handley Cross*.

In these chapters Jorrocks leads off by inviting Ego (who is clearly recognizable throughout as Nimrod) to visit his hounds and have a day with them. The letter of invitation sets the tone for the rest. It begins:

DEAR MR HEGO,

If your intercourse with Dukes and other great guns o' the world, leaves any margin for the doin's of the pop-guns o' the chase, I shall be werry 'appy if you will come here and take a look at our most provincial pack... *Entre nous*, as we say in France, I want to be famous, and you know how to do it. In course *mum's* the word.

> Yours to serve,
>
> JOHN JORROCKS.

P.S. Compts to Julius Seizeher and all the ancient Romans when you write.

Handley Cross, Chapter 50

Ego agrees to come. Jorrocks has a drag laid so as to ensure a hunt, the drag being finished off with a bag fox enlarged at the end of it in order to deceive Ego, just as he and Charrittie had done all those years ago at Boulogne. The ruse is briliantly successful. They have 'the greatest hunt that ever was seen' during which Ego, confronted by a stiff, fenced-up gap, tells Pigg he will hold his horse if Pigg gets down and pulls the rails out of the gap. 'Ar niver gets off!' Pigg snarls in reply and, sailing over the fence, leaves Ego standing and stranded. Refusing to take the fence or, in the argot of the day, 'cutting it' or 'funking it' Ego loses the hunt, fails even to come up at a check and is late at the kill after hounds have run into their fox and bowled him over in the open.

'Where's H'Ego?' enquires Jorrocks, and, comments Surtees, 'Ego answered "Where?"' Eventually he does cast up:

Up comes Ego, and Mr Jorrocks ... greets him ... 'Allow me, Mr Pomponius Hego', says he, 'to present you with the brush of the werry gamest old thief o' the world whatever was seen. Time, one hour and twenty minutes, with only one check—distance, wot you please to call it. Am sorry you weren't hup to see the darlins run into the warmint! Did it in style!' ... So saying, Mr Jorrocks, resuming his equilibrium, presented Ego with the brush, who received it with laudable condescension.

'Now, vot will you do?' inquired Mr Jorrocks; 'eat your sandwiches and find another fox, or eat your sandwiches and cut away 'ome?'

'Why, for my part, I should like to try again,' replied Ego; 'but I fear your horse's condition is hardly equal to another burst ...'

Handley Cross, Chapter 51

There is much more in the same strain and Surtees was to make it worse by going on to include a cruel parody of Nimrod's style at its most turgid and flowery in his account of 'A Day with Mr Jorrocks's Hounds, by Pomponius Ego'. This account contains the clear implication that Nimrod was writing up a run his cowardice across country had prevented him from seeing, and that he knew little of the subject upon which he was pontificating. The whole thing held Nimrod up to public ridicule as a funker, a fool, and a journalist who reported what he had not seen. It was a flagrant libel upon him both as a rider and a writer.

Surtees must have known very well just how unfair and unjust he was being. As recently as a year or so back Nimrod had gone with the best across his own northern countries and had probably never in his life turned away from a jumpable fence. The accusation of cowardice came especially badly from a man who, for his part, could probably count on the fingers of one hand the number of times he had jumped a fence in front during the whole of his hunting career.

The only possible justification that can be advanced for Surtees's writing as he did is that, as has been said, he never really appreciated the wounds his words could leave and that on this occasion he did believe, or at least persuaded himself, that he had a grievance against Nimrod for leaving the *New Sporting* and writing as he had done to *Bell's Life,* and that he took this means of redressing it. If so the riposte was out of all proportion to the offence. The results on publication were not to leave either Surtees or the book unscathed.

Surtees was still at odds with Ackermann who had indeed further increased their estrangement by acquiring from Spiers the copyright of *Jorrocks's Jaunts and Jollities.* This he was preparing to reissue with illustrations by Henry Alken without reference being made or royalty paid to Surtees, so it was that he sought Lockhart's advice about a publisher. He also asked Lockhart if he would allow the book to be dedicated to him. Lockhart wrote back:

All I can say is that if I had a book to bring out I should offer it to Bentley or Colburn, and ask him to give me an offer which I should then consider . . . I am extremely proud of your offer to me [of the dedication]—but flattering as it would be to receive such a compliment from you I feel great difficulty about it . . . I have an unfinished article by me touching the old Jorrocks, and shall hope to finish it and include the Club book [i.e. *Handley Cross* as yet untitled] as well as the 'Jollities and Jaunts.' But I think you would be tying my wrists by anything in the shape of a dedication . . . In short—but I know you will understand a nod as well as you would a wink.[6]

Literary log-rolling was not unknown then as now.

On receiving this letter Surtees sent the completed sheets to Henry Colburn who, as we have seen, had the gravest doubts about publishing. He thought the book too long and too rambling (which it was and is) and he was of the opinion, accurately as it turned out, that the notion of a cockney grocer as MFH would not be acceptable to the majority of readers at the time. He suggested cutting Jorrocks out of the book altogether for he thought him 'too coarse'. This aspersion on his favourite character was indignantly repudiated by Surtees and he refused for a moment to consider it. Still doubtful, Colburn sent the printed sheets to his literary adviser, William Sholbert, whose report is worth reproducing in full:

1st. Put name to work.

2nd. Attend to Mr C's suggestions for improving and curtailing the work.

3rdly. The story is meagre. Prune down a little of the coarseness of the fox-hunting grocer—Character of Mrs Barnaby (change the name) should be brought more prominently forward—rival doctors disposed of much too soon—omit any personalities such as Pomponius Ego (Mr Apperley)—Omit certain jokes and trivial passages here and there.[7]

When he received the report Colburn sent it on to Surtees. Having read it Surtees refused to discard the cloak of anonymity, an attitude he was to persist in all his life. None of his books or writings save the legal textbook ever appeared over his own name and he took pains to persecute most people, though not all as we shall see, who publicly revealed it. At one time he explained his attitude by saying 'an author is a troublesome character in the country'. Yet he never concealed his authorship from his friends and neighbours, openly acknowledging his books and freely giving away presentation copies. Perhaps a better clue to his reasons for insisting on anonymity is contained in a letter to Ainsworth when, as his editor, he made the same suggestion: 'I find', wrote Surtees, 'That I can write far better and with far more pleasure to myself when I am free to deny authorship if I like.'[8] Although he never, if it came to controversy, did take the step of denying authorship and hiding behind anonymity, which would have been entirely foreign to his nature, this sentence does give some key to his strange and contradictory character. He wanted success and enjoyed the limelight but it had to be limelight on a stage and amongst characters of his own choosing.

That the story of *Handley Cross* was and is meagre no one can deny. Surtees despised plots and went so far as to maintain with satisfaction in his preface to a later novel, *Ask Mamma,* 'It may be a recommendation to the lover of light literature to be told that the following story does not involve the complication of a plot.' No longer did he have to rely on his pen for a living; he was a squire and a sportsman, dashing off his books as he pleased and for his own pleasure, the inspired amateur for whom there was no necessity to bow to literary convention. Had it been otherwise the books might have been better and recognition come to him sooner. Unlike his great contemporary, Dickens, he never learnt, because he never had to, that what exists in print between stiff covers must have some essential form and coherence. Dickens, as Chesterton says of the *Pickwick Papers,* 'Tries to tell ten stories at once . . . sticks in irrelevant short stories shamelessly, as into a scrap-book; he adopts designs and abandons them, begins episodes and leaves them unfinished'. Those words might as well have been written about Surtees for they exactly describe his work. But, Chesterton goes on to say of Dickens, 'Dickens, like every other honest and effective writer, came at last to some degree of care and self-restraint. He learnt how to make his *dramatis personae* assist his drama; he learnt how to write stories which were full of rambling and perversity, but which were stories . . .'[9]

Surtees never learnt that self-restraint. He rambled on as he wished, discursing here and there not only on the technicalities of sport but on agriculture, drainage, the changing attitudes of the squirearchy, the iniquity of racing, especially of steeplechasing, or any other of the many foibles and crotchets then occupying his ever-active mind. Always he affected an offhand and patrician attitude to the writer's trade. 'Writing,' he said in *Hawbuck Grange,* the most discursive and disjointed of all his books, 'we imagine is something like smoking—men get into the way of it and can't leave it off. Like smoking it serves to beguile an idle hour. Individually speaking, writing makes us tolerably independent both of the world and the weather. We are never regularly high and dry for want of a companion so long as we can get pen, ink and paper.'

The fact that Mr Sholbert, a literary adviser and not a hunting man, instantly recognized Apperley in the portrait of Pomponius Ego and passed stricture upon it, did give Surtees cause to think. In consequence he cut Ego out entirely from the court scene but he was very reluctant to remove or alter the chapters concerning Ego's day with Mr Jorrocks. This is understandable for not only did they give him the opportunity of settling, as he thought, a score with Nimrod, but they are, in addition, if one overlooks the spiteful nature of the caricature, very well done and no doubt he had much enjoyed writing them. Also they contain one of the best of the many descriptions of a hunt which he ever wrote and some memorable Jorrocksiana:

'OLD 'ARD!' roars he to the forward roadsters, who are now getting among the hounds, 'You 'air-dresser on the chestnut 'oss!' holloaing to a gentleman with very big ginger whiskers; 'PRAY 'OLD 'ARD!'

'HAIR-DRESSER!' exclaims the gentleman, in a fury, turning short round; *'I'm an officer in the ninety-first regiment!'*

'Then you hossifer in the ninety-fust regiment, wot looks like an 'air-dresser, 'old 'ard,' replied Mr Jorrocks, trotting on . . .

Handley Cross, Chapter 51

Once more therefore he turned to Lockhart for advice. Lockhart was, in fact, the last person whose counsel he should have sought on a question of defamation of character, literary or otherwise. For Lockhart had not entirely cast aside the taste for invective with which he had enlivened *Blackwood's* in his unregenerate days, and he still thrived on controversy. Despite constant pleas from his father-in-law to restrain his barbed pen he could on occasion let fly in the *Quarterly* with all his former ferocity. It was only a year or so back that he had written such an excoriating review of one of Tennyson's early works as to silence the poet for ten years.

Having read the chapters and, as might have been expected from one of his temperament and inclinations, having thoroughly enjoyed them, Lockhart wrote back: 'Leave the Nimrod part to me; only let me have the sheet he figures in and I can do it without offence to either party.'[10] Just what he meant by this arcane utterance is far from clear unless he was referring to the review promised in the 'nod is as good as a wink' sentence in his former letter. Surtees, however, took it as confirming that these chapters were permissible in print and he returned the book to Colburn without further deletions.

Colburn still hesitated. Lockhart's aid was called in again by Surtees and Lockhart in response urged its merits on Colburn, pressing him to publish. Yielding to the influence from this august and powerful quarter, Colburn at length decided to go ahead, and submitted a profit-sharing contract to Surtees for signature. There was a wrangle over terms for Surtees objected to certain provisions for deductions and expenses which Colburn had inserted to protect himself. Eventually this was cleared up and on 30 July 1842 the contract for 'A sporting novel, to consist of three volumes, post 8vo, the title of which is to be mutually agreed on', was signed by both parties.[11]

Surtees, wisely, wanted the book to be illustrated in the fashion of the time, the 'three-deckers' of Dickens, Thackeray, and Trollope all containing plates by established artists. He himself approached Hablot K. Browne (Phiz) who had illustrated the first edition of the *Jaunts and Jollities*. Phiz knew horses and could draw them which was, of course, an essential requirement. He agreed to carry out the work but as the foremost and most sought-after illustrator of the day he was at the time inundated with commissions. He kept procrastinating over delivery of the plates, finally excusing himself altogether on the grounds that he had too much work on his hands and in any event the payment offered—£45—was inadequate for an artist of his standing and reputation. Colburn then tried to interest John Leech but Leech was busy with work for *Punch* and the fee he demanded was in Colburn's opinion much too high for the expected sale of the book. Having failed with Leech, Colburn then approached George Tattersall ('Wildrake' of the *New Sporting*). Their negotiations appeared to be going well when a complication arose. Lockhart had, before publication and from sheets supplied to him by Surtees, written a long and laudatory review of the book and he was anxious to use it. The discussions with the various artists over illustrations had already caused delay and postponement of the publication date. Both Surtees and Lockhart were becoming impatient, and Lockhart intimated to Colburn that the review would appear in the March 1843 issue of the *Quarterly* or not at all. Much, Colburn thought, if not everything, depended on the review. He therefore abandoned all thoughts of illustrations and went ahead. 'There can be little fear', he wrote to Surtees, 'of disposing of the first edition of 750 copies which have been printed.'[12]

Lockhart's review, unstinted in its praise, duly appeared; the only qualifying sentence, which was read as the slightest tap on Surtees's wrist for his treatment of Nimrod, ran 'He might, if he pleased, take a high place among our modern novelists...We advise him to try his hand—and that before he loses the high spirits of youth;—but he must, in so doing, by all means curb his propensity to caricature.'[13]

This, presumably, is what he meant by his former remark 'Leave Nimrod to me.' If he thought that this mildest of rebukes would be sufficient to mollify Nimrod and to save 'giving offence to either party' both he and Surtees were to be speedily disillusioned. It is notable, too, that throughout the review he referred to Surtees by name, thus revealing his closely guarded anonymity, and that Surtees issued no rebuke for this presumption, a concession he was not to extend to other less favoured and less powerful editors and reviewers.

Another notice of the book appeared about the same time, on this occasion in the *Sunday Times*. The reviewer had picked up the obvious reference to Nimrod and he commented on it. Nimrod happened to be in London just then, staying at 20 Upper Belgrave Place where he was undergoing treatment for an internal injury caused by a bad fall when his horse, on getting up, trod on his stomach. He read the *Sunday Times* the day it was issued, realized that the passages referred to in the review must contain a scurrilous attack on him and that the name alone, 'Pomponius Ego', was both insulting and defamatory. Immediately he wrote to Surtees as follows:

SIR,—In a notice of your 'Handley Cross' novel in the 'Sunday Times' of yesterday I find the following paragraph: 'There is little of a personal nature in this entertaining production; that little is confined to a full-length portrait of Nimrod described as Pomponius Ego. The picture, though highly-coloured, is utterly unmistakable.' I feel myself called upon to demand, on your part, an *immediate* avowal or contradiction of this presumed fact.—Your obedt. Servt.,

CHAS JAS APPERLEY.

Surtees's reply was instant and uncompromising:

DURHAM.

SIR,—Yours of the 27th has just reached me here, where I have been staying. In reply to your demand, I beg to say the character of P. Ego is meant for Nimrod.—Your obedt. Servt.,

R.S.S.
March 30th/43.

Just the same he had obviously taken some pains over concocting this reply for in the draft the words 'the enquiry' are crossed out and 'your demand' substituted.

Having received this dusty answer Nimrod's reply was equally prompt and to the point:

SIR,—I have received your letter avowing the fact imputed to you by the 'S. Times'.

Not having seen your book beyond the parts quoted in the 'Quarterly Review' and the 'S. Times', I am, of course, unable to say

105

more on the subject until I have read the part relating to myself, which I shall take an early opportunity of doing, and of addressing myself to you again.—Your obedt. Servt.

CHAS JAS APPERLEY.[14]

It now looked very much as if Surtees was about to suffer the indignity of being called out by a man old enough to be his father whom he had gratuitously insulted in print. He certainly thought so, for he franked the envelope containing the letter, 'Nimrod's challenge'. In the dilemma in which he found himself he sought advice as he had done before over the affair with Carleton. In no way could the issue be avoided on social grounds as had happened with Carleton—not that, once it was joined, he would have wanted to—for Nimrod's standing in society was every bit as good as his own. It is just possible, however, that the reason he sought advice was that for once it was being brought home to him that he had pushed his desire to hurt far beyond the bounds of reasonable mockery. After all, Mr Sholbert, the literary adviser, had thought the chapters should be omitted altogether, even Lockhart with his love of a literary slanging match had issued a gentle warning and now the reviewer in the *Sunday Times,* a total stranger, had picked the matter up. It was to his old friend Hodgson Hinde, for whom as we know Surtees had acted in a similar matter some years before, that he now turned to ask for counsel. Hinde wrote back:

22 PARK STREET, GROSVENOR SQUARE,
1st April 1843.

MY DEAR SURTEES,—Most certainly I did not notice anything in your work, which I have read, personally offensive to Apperley...He has no right to find fault with your caricature of his egotistical style, nor with his giving a minute description of a day's sport of which he has seen little. I think it is probable you will hear no more of him, but if you do, I shall be here till the day before Good Friday, when I go to Dover.—Yours,

J. H. H.[15]

Hinde was inclined to treat these 'matters of honour' in a cavalier fashion and one can only conclude from this letter that he knew little of either hunting or journalism, for to read into those chapters 'his giving a minute description of a day's sport of which he has seen little' was to confirm the libel both on Nimrod's ability as a horseman and integrity as a correspondent. Nor can he have read *Handley Cross* itself very thoroughly, for did not Surtees himself make Mr Jorrocks say in his very first Sportin' Lector: 'Well did that great man, I think it was Walter Scott, but if it war'nt, 'twas little Bartley, the bootmaker, say, that there was no young man that would not rather have a himputation on his morality than on his 'ossmanship.' (*Handley Cross,* Chapter 18). Nimrod was not a young man but he had remained young in heart and the 'himputation' with all its hurtful implications stood out bare and undisguised in those chapters.

It is said that Nimrod did in fact issue a challenge. If he did the consequences might have been serious for Surtees since Nimrod, old and ill though he was, numbered amongst his other accomplishments that of being a crack shot, not that that was likely to deter Surtees from accepting it once he had convinced himself that his cause was just. The issue of a challenge cannot, however, be either confirmed or denied since any subsequent correspondence, if it existed at all, has been either lost or was destroyed by Surtees. In any event nothing further materialized for within a month Nimrod suffered an attack of peritonitis and on 17 May he died, his end hastened by the effects of his fall. Nor were his last days made any happier by the anguish of mind caused by the incident. And, as Surtees was to find out, his ghost was not going to be easily laid.

CHAPTER SEVEN

The Failure of *Handley Cross*

THE sales of *Handley Cross* did not come up even to Colburn's meagre anticipations for he failed to sell out the small first edition he had printed, only disposing of a few score of copies. Within six months of publication, glad to be shut of an enterprise he had mistrusted from the start, he cut his losses and sold off his remaining stock to Rudolph Ackermann, who was in turn unsuccessful in finding a market for them and had them left on his hands.

It has been said that the lack of illustrations killed any hope of success the book might have had, so that not even Lockhart's laudatory review could save it. It is the case that the omission of illustrations did militate against the book; it is also true that Lockhart's laudations were less effective than his denunciations, and in any event the august *Quarterly* rarely reached the sporting public except on such rare occasions as when it was enhanced by contributions from Nimrod's pen. But the real reasons why the book failed lay far deeper.

The success or failure of a novel often depends upon how well it chimes with the social climate of the day. The arrival of John Jorrocks, grocer, as MFH, was something quite new on the sporting and social scene, and quite foreign to the accepted convention of what a Master of Foxhounds should be. In the mid-nineteenth century MFHs stood high in the hierarchy of class. Many, if not most, were aristocrats, those that were not were landed gentlemen. Osbaldeston acquired the sobriquet 'Squire' because he was the first commoner to hunt the Quorn Hounds for many years. When Leicestershire was full of the sprigs of nobility hunting its other packs, to take a mere grocer and a garrulous, self-made, tippling one at that, who gloried in his origins—his mother was a washer-woman—who treated aristocrats, 'swells', and 'sojer Hossifers' to the rough edge of his ready tongue, and who pontificated at length on the art and science of venery in a series of semi-literate 'lectors' founded on Beckford whose tenets he knew by heart, and to make such a man an MFH was arrant heresy and an affront to all right-thinking members of the hunting classes.

'What's the meaning of Jorrocks?' Captain Freeman, a friend of Surtees's, Master of the Southwold and later of the Old Berkeley, who might well, Surtees said, have stood for a model of Jorrocks himself, commented to him, adding: 'I don't understand that Jorrocks'.[1] He was only putting into words the thoughts of the few who attempted to read the book and found themselves floundering in it.

The character of Jorrocks together with the whole tone of the book was, as Sholbert had pointed out, tainted with that 'coarseness' so abhorrent to the early-Victorian public. Under the young Queen tastes were changing very quickly and anything smacking of Regency raffishness and excess was looked upon askance. To dub a book 'coarse' was a damning label then and for many years to come. (Lockhart, oddly enough, who delighted in Jorrocks, found Pickwick 'all very well but damned low'.) In Surtees's case this damaging tag attached to his work was to persist long after his death. It was perpetuated in Thomas Seccombe's vignette in the *Dictionary of National Biography* published in 1892 in which, after patronizing Surtees (which would have brought swift reply had the author been alive), he refers slightingly to the 'coarseness of the text'.

It was unfortunate for Surtees, too, that one of the few *double entendres* to appear in his books occurs in the early chapters of *Handley Cross.* After the occasion inspiring the immortal 'COME HUP! I say, YOU HUGLY BEAST!' incident in which Jorrocks is deposited in a muddy ditch, he is hacking home through Handley Cross not in the best of tempers. In the street he is greeted with cries of derision from women and children.

Next as he passed the Barley-mow beer-shop, Mrs Gallon the landlady, who was nursing a child at the door, exclaimed across the street, to Blash the barber's pretty but rather wordy wife—

'*A—a—a!* ar say Fanny!—old fatty's had a fall!'

To which Mrs Blash replied with a scornful toss of her head, at our now admiring friend—'*Hut!* he's always on his back, that old feller.'

'Not 'alf so often as you are, old gal!' retorted the now indignant Mr Jorrocks, spurring on out of hearing.

Handley Cross, Chapter 14

Pigg, too, with his drinking, his incomprehensible dialect, and his damn-your-eyes attitude to everyone, high and low, together with Benjamin, the useless and slothful boy, stealing marmalade and anything else he can lay his hands upon, were out of the ordinary run of smartly turned-out, forelock-touching hunt servants. Given the context of the times, therefore, there was some justification for the label 'coarse' being attached to the whole household, however hilarious their adventures and misadventures—mostly the latter—might be. In fact their creation was a truly original one and something approaching a stroke of genius but, unfortunately for Surtees, neither critics not public saw it that way nor were they to do so for many years to come.

Jorrocks was a throw-back to the earthier, lustier fictional texture of Fielding and Richardson. But the ears of the public, tuned to more delicate notes, failed to distinguish the comedy from the coarseness. They were mistaken; though it took him so long, he did come into his own after Surtees's death, when Jorrocks eventually came to be recognized as the great comic creation that he is, a character realized in the round, good-humoured, fallible, loyal to his servants, faithful to his friends, disrespectful to all, prepared to swop words with anyone be he marquess or milkman, and as English as old oak.

But, nevertheless, the public refused to take him to their hearts. Nurtured as they were on Nimrod's doctrine of dash and courage, his declarations that 'the pace was too good to enquire' when a friend had a fall, and his exhortations to 'throw your heart over in front', what were they to make of a Master who publicly declared, 'Vot a huntsman I should be if it wasn't for the leaps', that a fall was 'a hawful thing', and, in elaboration, 'a great sixteen 'and 'oss lyin' on one like a blanket, or sittin' with his monstrous hemispheres on one's chest; sendin' one's werry soul out o' one's nostrils! Dreadful thought! Vere's the brandy?'[2]

Accustomed, too, to the placing of an MFH on a pedestal far above his fellows and a lord only a step or two below the Almighty, how could they understand this Master who announced to his hearers: 'Arter all's said and done there are but two sorts of folk in the world, Peerage folks, and Post Hoffice Directory folks, and its the Post Hoffice Directory folks wot pays their bills . . . I'm a Post Hoffice Directory man not a Peerage man.' And who then went even further: 'Have no great fancy for lords—werry apt to make first a towel, and then a dish clout of one'.[3] Surtees appears to have appreciated this after his own fashion for in his preface to the first impression—which was later excised from subsequent editions—he gave hostages to fortune by flatly stating in his own uncompromising way: 'Once and for all then let us state that it is *not* a genteel work,— not one of our Lord *Jeems* [James] silver-fork school of writing, but a mere tale of ordinary, tradesman-like sporting life.'

But there was another reason for the failure of *Handley Cross* which has been largely overlooked. Surtees had made too many enemies. His winged words in those hunting reports were now coming home to roost. Those who had been hurt or scarred by them were unlikely to buy the book or, if they did, to do other than join in the current disparagement of it. And, as well, Nimrod had left behind him numerous friends and many affectionate memories. He had been too well liked and admired for his courage, character, and the dash and fire of his writing for Surtees's traducing of a dying man to pass without adverse comment. In addition to the Pomponius Ego chapters there are at least eleven other references to Nimrod in *Handley*

Cross, all either sneering or slighting. His friends, who were legion throughout the whole sporting world not only in England but in France, did not overlook this when Surtees and his book came up for discussion 'across the mahogany' or when the port was passing.

Nor did the new edition of the *Jaunts and Jollities* fare any better than *Handley Cross* when Ackermann reissued it. Even the splendid set of Alken prints which he commissioned as illustrations failed to move it, though they were, and are, marvellous conversation pieces in their own right. The mortification suffered by Surtees as a result of these failures cannot have been lessened by the fact that Nimrod's only novel, *The Life of A Sportsman,* a far inferior work to his and forgotten now, which was published by Ackermann the year before, was selling well and proving universally popular.

Jorrocks was Surtees's favourite character. He was determined not to allow him to perish and so, undeterred, he set himself to constructing a further book about him.

Hillingdon Hall proved, if anything, an even greater failure than the previous two books and is, with justification, the least read of all his novels. The reason is not far to seek. Surtees took Jorrocks from the only milieu where he was truly at home—the hunting-field—and transmogrified him into a cockney squire grappling with the problems of farming an estate, dealing with the changing face of agriculture, and assuming the rights and duties appurtenant to the position of landed proprietor.

Surtees's range as a writer was extremely narrow; he could only fulfil himself when dealing with those subjects which passionately interested him—horses, hounds, and hunting, or the social mores of country houses and those who inhabited them, be they masters or servants. When dealing with these he could fire his pages with his own enthusiasm for the chase, and fascination with the characteristics of those who followed it. The mechanics of houses great and not so great were, too, to him a source of endless interest and sardonic amusement which he could convey to his readers. Once he strayed from those familiar grounds he lost his touch, and his skills in drawing character or, more accurately, caricature, to a large extent deserted him.

In *Hillingdon Hall* Jorrocks, now aged sixty-five, has given up hounds; Pigg and Benjamin both reappear in various guises but they are shadows of their former selves. Mrs Jorrocks comes more into her own along with Mrs Flather as the first and most formidable pair of Surtees's match-making mothers. Indeed the most telling scene in the book and one worthy of Trollope at his best is where Mrs Flather confronts the Duke and Duchess of Donkeyton on the subject of the Marquis of Bray, their son and heir, having trifled with her daughter's affections. But by and large the book is only a vehicle for carrying Surtees's reflections on the state of agriculture in Durham, with special emphasis on his pet obsession, drainage, for fulminating against the anti-Corn Law agitation then at its height, and for exploiting his experiences on the Bench (Jorrocks becomes a JP) and when fighting an election for, unlike Surtees himself, Jorrocks fights and wins a seat, ending up as an MP by defeating no less than the Marquis of Bray by two votes.

The book comes briefly to life when Jorrocks, encouraged by Pigg, has his last day's hunting with a scratch pack of harriers. Confronted by an insurmountable stone wall and thinking he knows the run of the hare, he leaves his horse with a shepherd and proceeds on foot. Soon he is blown and has a severe stitch in his side. He sees hounds growing 'small by degrees, and beautifully less' (yet another of Surtees's misquotations)—and fails to keep in touch.

'It's no use,' repeated he with a melancholy shake of the head. 'It's all U.P. with J.J. Ah!' continued he, *'age will tell! I never thought to come to this,'* added he with a deep sigh. 'I'm gettin' an *old* man,' said he, in a low tone, as he laid his hand on the wall to hoist himself up ... 'They von't ketch her,' grunted Mr Jorrocks to himself, lowering himself down the wall, thinking he might chance to see the finish ... As if to thwart our friend hounds took to running as soon as he got established on his legs and had started

into an involuntary trot. It was, however, a very short one. The stitch in his side soon returned, and in less than two minutes our old friend was *hors de combat.*

'There's an end of *my* 'unting,' said he, dropping on to a large stone and bursting into tears.

Hillingdon Hall, Chapter 31

It was indeed a sad finish to the hunting career of the most famous of all Masters of Foxhounds.

Even in *Hillingdon Hall,* however, there are flashes of the old rogue in his finest form, rumbustious, vulgar, and unrepentant. At the dinner party at Donkeyton Castle, dressed, we are told, 'in the full-dress uniform of the Handley Cross Hunt—sky-blue coat, lined with pink silk; canary-coloured shorts, and white silk stockings', almost the first thing he informs the Duke is, 'Where I dine I sleep, and where I sleep I breakfast, your Greece', remarking also in passing when the Duke enquires if he would show him his room, that, if Mrs Jorrocks 'wasn't long gone he'd be bound to say he'd run her to ground by her scent, she musked herself so uncommon 'igh when she went to fine places'.[4]

Not surprisingly in view of this and other similar instances such as Jorrocks drinking both the Duke and himself virtually insensible over the port, the taint of 'coarseness' was once more attributed to the book and used as evidence to brand Surtees's work as unacceptable to all refined and right-thinking people. Surtees was not alone among authors in suffering in this way. At much the same time Harriet Martineau, a writer in a very different vein, was complaining: 'Youths and ladies in those days looked for lords and ladies in every page of a new novel.'[5] Moreover their 'lords' must be *preux chevaliers* without fear or fault and their 'ladies' without shadow of *reproche,* a need which Frank Smedley and Whyte-Melville were shortly to fulfil in their hunting novels, thus setting back Surtees's chances of success still further. There were lords all right in *Hillingdon Hall* but they were very far from being Bayards. The Marquis of Bray was a fop and a fool, and as for his father:

The Failure of Handley Cross

The Duke of Donkeyton was a thick-headed, self-sufficient old man—one who thought that everybody must like what he liked —and who could not make allowances for the different tastes difference of age produces . . . Now and then His Grace unbent and did a little popularity as we have seen him on the occasion of Mr Jorrocks's visit . . . but he soon relapsed into his former stateliness, after having offended as many by his blunders and want of tact as he pleased by his laboured condescension.

Hillingdon Hall, Chapter 11

Worse still, this was an all too recognizable portrait of the then Duke of Northumberland who instantly struck the Surtees family off his list of acquaintances.

Hillingdon Hall first ran as a serial in the *New Sporting* from February 1843 to June 1844 when, for some unknown reason, it was abruptly cut short at chapter eleven and left unfinished. The serial contained seven uncoloured plates, four of them by Wildrake and the remainder by Henry Heath. As illustrations they were undistinguished, and perhaps for that reason when Henry Colburn, surprisingly in view of the failure of *Handley Cross,* agreed to publish it in book form he once more omitted the plates. In 1845, Surtees having then added the remaining chapters, it came out in three volumes under Colburn's imprint. It was an utter failure and Colburn was left with most of the stock on his hands.

The book was far too much of a tract to have had any real chance of success. The year before it was published Surtees had become a leading member of a local committee set up to fight the anti-Corn Law agitation, and he was also active in the Northumberland Society for the Protection of British Agriculture. He was always a passionate fighter for causes he believed to be right and in the book he had allowed himself to be carried away by the opportunity it afforded him of propagating his current convictions and obsessions. Lacking, as a writer, the self-discipline to control these outpourings he ruined his book and in the process lost most of the fun and humour which had permeated *Handley Cross* to its immense advantage and ultimate salvation.

By the time the book was published Surtees was heart and soul the Squire of Hamsterley. As well as his committee work and looking after the family's not inconsiderable farming, colliery, and other interests, he had for some years been vice-president of the County Durham Conservative Association. In addition in 1843 he had accepted a commission as major in the Durham militia. It can only have been a sense of duty which impelled him to take this step for all his life he scorned soldiers and soldiering, invariably holding them both up to derision in his books. The ''AIR-DRESSER on the chestnut 'oss,' is only one example of many: there were the 'Cut 'em Down Captains' dragged into *Handley Cross* for the sole purpose of making fun of them, and did not Mr Jorrocks say in one of his lectors, 'The dragon soger officer is the most dangerous, and may be known by the viskers under his nose. A foot soger officer's 'oss is generally better in his wind than on his legs. They generally wear chin wigs, and always swear the leaps are nothin' compared with those in the county they come from—Cheapside, p'raps.'[6]

But the cruellest of his soldier-portraits are those of Colonel Blunt, a dishonest and dishonourable buffoon, and Major Fibs, a rascally horse-coping cavalryman who felt 'morally certain he was equal to easing Tom [Hall] of any superfluous cash he might happen to have, as he had eased many a youngster both in his regiment and out of it'. Both Colonel Blunt and Major Fibs are members of the Heavyside Dragoons, the regiment which plays a considerable part in *Young Tom Hall*. As always Surtees put the experience he had gained in the militia to telling use in his unforgiving and savage caricature of a dissolute, non-sporting cavalry regiment, the officers of which were 'not even uniform in their uniforms, consequently little could be expected of them out of it'. Such was his description of them as he lampooned their appearance at a meet of the Heartycheer Hounds which they attended solely with the intention of consuming the free and elaborate breakfast provided.[7]

Two years after he joined, a letter came from the Horse

Guards asking the colonel of the regiment whether in the event of war his officers were prepared to serve overseas. Immediately Surtees took the opportunity offered. Indicating that his extensive interests and obligations would not permit him to sign on for foreign service he resigned his commission. He had never been an enthusiastic soldier. 'Though a Major of Militia I never had a sword on', he wrote to Mark Lemon some years afterwards.[8] But his scenes from military life when they appeared in *Young Tom Hall* cannot have endeared him to his former comrades-in-arms.

All these activities may well have hindered his writing and they unquestionably inhibited him from adopting a professional attitude to the art and craft of the novel, but they did not stop him, nor was he deterred by failure. He wrote standing up, at a small short-legged desk set on a table. Once started he would work throughout the day not even ceasing for the meals his family was commanded to bring up to him. Although his writing, at least at first sight, appears as slapdash as his construction (and much of it is), it is evident that it did not come easily to him. Over some of it at least, especially the dialogue, he took immense pains and his manuscripts are full of deletions, substitutions, alterations, and rewriting. From these it is clear that he was always striving for the feeling of spontaneity and naturalness that imbues his prose at its best and makes his dialogues such a delight. As is so often the case with him, easy reading did not mean easy writing. But in 1845 he had not yet found either his *métier* or his market, and his next effort in book form was really only expanded journalism.

CHAPTER EIGHT

Hack-work and *Hawbuck Grange*

The Analysis of the Hunting Field was the somewhat grandiloquent title bestowed on the new book. Like his legal textbook
it was a technical work, in this case devoted to the theory and
practice of hunting and huntsmen, illuminated by character
sketches of those types most likely to be met with in the
hunting field. Although it contains much sound common
sense based on the eternal verities of the chase it has,
inevitably, dated, and its main interest now is the revealing
insights it discloses into the mind and character of the man
who wrote it, his attitude to underlings, the other sex, and the
social mores of his time.

Surtees was one of those writers who could commit nothing
to paper without stamping his personality upon it. 'If half the
fellows calling themselves "grooms" were in their proper
places how well the pigs would be attended to!' was how he
opened his chapter on the subject of stable servants;[1] and he
could never prevent humour breaking in as in his advice to an
MFH on the correct and polite way in which he should
remonstrate with one who is overriding his hounds: 'First he
should cry out, as hard as he can, "Hold Hard!" If anyone
should persist after that he begins moderately at first and says,
"I beg you, sir, will you stop your horse. Pray, sir, stop; God bless you,
sir, stop; *God d—n your blood, sir,* stop your horse!"'[2]

Then there are his mordant reflections on the opposite sex.
He was firmly of the opinion, 'I don't like to see women with
foxhounds; a man does not like riding before them, or leaving
them in the lurch; and even if they do "go along" the whole
field is kept in alarm lest an accident happen.' Women out
hunting, too, he said, 'are generally desperate tuft-hunters.

There is no denying that tuft-hunting is an instinct that prevails over nearly the whole sex. They are as much in their place at the meet as they are out of it tearing across country . . . one of our objections to ladies hunting, though we do not know that we have ever seen it taken before is that it deprives gentlemen of the agreeable change and variety which their society makes in the evening.' However he had to admit: 'When women do ride they generally ride like the very devil. There is no medium with them. They either "go" to beat the men, or they don't go at all. We have seen some uncommon performers among women, performers that would put nine tenths of the men to the blush. . . .'[3] Later he goes on to consider the hunting field as a mart for marriage, illustrating his views by a long parable concerning Henrietta Cotton-wool's pursuit of Sir Rasper Smashgate. (Surtees, incidentally, here and elsewhere could never rid himself of the pestilential Victorian habit of using heavy-handed onomatopoeic names for his characters—Captain Shabbyhounde, Lord Hearty-cheer, Mr Lampoil, groom of the chambers, Mr Queencake, the confectioner, Lord Lionel Lazytongs are only a few, though it is noticeable that in his best books they are either absent or so toned down, as in Lucy Glitters and Sir Harry Scattercash, as to be fitting and effective.)

'A man is not a match for a woman until he is married,' Surtees says in the course of this parable, a sentiment he repeats in *Ask Mamma* later on. There were few vocations open to Victorian young women other than matrimony and Surtees made the ruthless pursuit of the male by one or more of them and their mothers the theme of several of his books during which both mother and daughter were held up to merciless ridicule, for the chase almost invariably ended in humiliating failure. Again it is notable that this theme is sublimated into a very minor part in his two best books, *Mr Sponge's Sporting Tour* and *Mr Facey Romford's Hounds,* in which his heroines spring not from the respectable classes but from a delicious and endearing slice of the *demi-monde.*

The Analysis contains yet another unjustified and unjustifi-

119

able backhander at Nimrod who was, of course, now far beyond taking any earthly retribution. In the course of one of the chapters Surtees flatly stated that Nimrod had not written the article 'The Chace' for the *Quarterly* at all but that Lockhart had been responsible for it in its entirety. 'Since Mr Lockhart went down into Leicestershire with his good "little bay horse" and wrote the surprising article on the "Chase" in the *Quarterly Review*', he says, 'people have been rather suspicious of strangers in the hunting-field . . .'[4] This unqualified ascription of the article to Lockhart and denial of Nimrod's authorship was all the more remarkable and reprehensible in that while at work on *The Analysis* Surtees was writing for the magazine Ainsworth had founded a year or so back and was publishing under his own name a long, five-part, critical and biographical study of Nimrod and his works. It is hardly necessary to state that in this study it was the critical element which was preponderant. It is in fact a vicious and spiteful *mélange* of denigration, insinuation, and derogation of Nimrod's abilities both as a horseman and a writer and, on Surtees's part, self-justification for his own actions in the many arguments, controversies, and accusations he had launched against its subject during his lifetime, with special reference to the Pomponius Ego affair. In this study, although he hints at it he does not go so far as to make without qualification the libellous assertion contained in the book.

On Nimrod's death Surtees had written a restrained but patronizing obituary for the *New Sporting*. While it contained none of the venom with which he had attacked its subject during his lifetime it nevertheless did him scant justice and did little to assuage the wrath of Nimrod's friends. Now, at the end of the articles in *Ainsworth's Magazine,* for reasons known only to himself, he reprinted this notice in full. If it was intended to be some sort of palliative to what had gone before then it was a singularly feeble one. Nor did Surtees cease thereafter in his books and writings to sneer and snipe at Nimrod and his attitude to fox-hunting. After his death in the notes he left behind him there were further jottings for more attacks.

It is impossible to avoid the conclusion that Surtees, self-absorbed, introspective, misanthropic, was obsessively jealous of Nimrod's sporting, social, and literary successes. Surtees's books were failures, his two years of hunting hounds had ended in rows and bitterness, nor had he shown outstanding sport when he had them; he lacked, and he must have known it, both the nerve and horsemanship to cross a big—or any other—country, brilliantly; his one attempt at entering Parliament had ended in defeat. As against this Nimrod's career as a horseman, a writer, and a 'goer' over the grass countries had flared like a comet. Vindictiveness and uncharitableness of this strength and nature so violently expressed have a way of being self-defeating, and some years later when Surtees was trying to get a second edition of *Handley Cross* off the ground, he found the shade of Nimrod still haunting him and, to some extent at least, taking its revenge.

When *The Analysis* had ended its serial run Surtees had to look for a publisher. Colburn was no longer interested but the break with Ackermann had been at least temporarily healed since Ackermann had made due obeisance and apology a year or so back, writing to Surtees:

DEAR SIR,—I am exceedingly sorry there has been a little difference between us these last few years; I do hope and trust you will overlook it and not think anything more about it, and anything I can do to merit your approbation in the future will give me the greatest pleasure...[5]

So Surtees turned to his old friend and colleague for publication. Ackermann brought the book out in 1846 handsomely illustrated with a set of coloured plates by Henry Alken. Even these, however, could not move it and it had, as indeed might have been expected, a very limited sale.

Surtees almost certainly thought of *The Analysis* as a stopgap work, as journalism turned hastily into book form which would keep his name as the author of *Handley Cross* before the public for, despite his passion for anonymity, he was very conscious of his readership. 'There is nearly an unoccupied field in illustrated sporting literature,' he wrote a little later to a publisher, 'the magazines being very few and expensive.' Indeed he thought Ackermann's pricing of *The Analysis* at a guinea and a half too expensive, and protested. To which Ackermann replied, 'I like the book; it is cheap, not dear' and, later in the correspondence, added the optimistic note: 'It will sell in time.'

His optimism was misplaced. In terms of sales *The Analysis* was yet another failure and Surtees took his next book, *Hawbuck Grange*, elsewhere. In this Ackermann was fortunate for *Hawbuck Grange* was an even greater failure than the others.

The title *Hawbuck Grange* was that under which, after much discussion, it was eventually published but it first appeared as a serial in *Bell's Life* under the title *Sporting Sketches*, beginning six months after the run of *The Analysis* ended. Ostensibly it concerns the hunting adventures of Tom Scott, a sporting farmer who insists on being dubbed 'Mister' not 'Esquire' —yet another example of Surtees's inverted snobbery: 'He had "THOMAS SCOTT, FARMER, HAWBUCK GRANGE" in honest parliamentary-sized letters, without flourish or eye-magnifying geegaw, on the back of his dog-cart as anyone who likes to inspect it may see.'[6] Scott is one of the few characters in all Surtees's books to be both decent and likeable. Had he taken the trouble to develop Scott's character and to mould the sketches into some semblance of coherence, *Hawbuck Grange* might have been a very good book indeed. The theme, if it has one, is that Tom is torn between hunting and matrimony and hunting keeps coming first.

The book begins brilliantly for it gives Surtees the opportunity of describing the sort of provincial pack of hounds—in this case, harriers—so dear to his heart in their unpretentiousness. This is the Goose and Dumpling Hunt, so called because of the staple fare served at its dinners after hunting. Once again, at the outset, Surtees takes the opportunity of harping on his creed concerning riding to hounds:

The members of the hunt are all real sportsmen, men who love hunting innately, but who take no pleasure in leaping. Indeed, to tell the truth, since Beanstack broke his collarbone by landing on a donkey instead of *terra firma,* on the far side of an unsurveyed fence, the members have declined 'extra risk', as the insurance offices say, and if there isn't a gap where they want to be over, why they make one.

Some people fancy hard riding an indispensable quality for a sportsman, but we believe if we were to canvass the sporting world, we should find the real lovers of hunting are anything but a hard-riding set . . .

Hawbuck Grange, Chapter 2

This, of course, is special pleading and unconvincing at that. It is merely an excuse for lack of nerve and, as the Nimrods of this world might well reply, has been used as such by pusillanimous masters and hunting correspondents down to this day, entirely overlooking the fact that those who show best sport and see most fun are those who ride up to their hounds.

Surtees shows how his sympathies were always with the hare who was not a cunning and clever predator as was the fox:

'We've been *walked* out,' replied Scott. 'Very true,' retorted Mr Trumper, 'very true,' repeated he, 'and that makes me think she won't be far off. Gad, sir, she's under your horse's nose at this moment!' added he. '*Hold hard!* while I draw the hounds off, or they'll spoil her.'

Trumper then drew the hounds away, and looking a little ahead Scott saw what at first sight looked like a clod, but which, on closer observation, proved to be poor puss . . .

'*Save her!*' whispered Scott, 'save her! she's a good 'un and will give us a gallop another day. Mercy's all that's wanting to make the sport perfect.'

Hawbuck Grange, Chapter 2

Afterwards Tom falls in for their hunt dinner, which Surtees describes in loving detail to show how the yeomen of England could do things when they tried. It was a far more appetizing and satisfying repast than many of the grand meals in great houses which he was later to describe in sardonic detail, course by pretentious course:

123

There are two things in this world that there is seldom any mistake about—the smell of a fox and the smell of a roast goose... The Rev Timothy Goodman having said grace they all set to with the most rapacious and vigorous determination.

For people who are fond of goose (and who is not?) a greater treat could not be devised. There was no taking the edge of the appetite off with soup, or fish, or patties, or cutlets, or side dishes of any sort; but they sat down to dine off the one thing they expected. This, too, was done in the fairest, most equitable way imaginable; for instead of a favoured few getting the breast and tit-bits, leaving nothing but grisly drumsticks for late comers, each man had his own half goose, and could take whatever part he liked first, without eating in haste and fear that the next favoured cut would be gone ere he could get at it again. All, too, dining off goose, and eating most profusely of stuffing, none could reproach the other with 'Smelling of onions.'

Silence appeared to be the order of the day both morning and evening, for with the exception of a voice occasionally hallooing out 'Beer!' scarce a word passed, until the dishes presented a most beggarly account of bones. Beer they might call it, and beer it might look like, being both light and bright, but it was uncommonly strong and heady to take...

Trumper, having made a most exemplary onslaught on his half goose, and washed it down with many potations of malt liquor, at last threw himself back in his semi-circular chair, and bellowed out the word 'BRANDY'. Mrs Trumper immediately dived into her pocket, and, beckoning to the maid, gave her the key of a cupboard formed of one corner of the room, from whence she produced a most liberal sized blue glass spirit-stand with the names, 'HOLLANDS', 'RUM', 'BRANDY', in gilt letters round the bottle necks.

'Take a thimbleful of brandy, Mr Scott, after your goose,' said Trumper appealing to our friend; and forthwith the little maid brought him a large wine glass on a *papier mâché* stand with a hare painted on the bottom, and proceeded to help him. 'Stop!' exclaimed Scott, when she had got it half filled.

'Nay,' roared Trumper in disgust. 'What's the top of the glass made for, d'ye think?—*fill it up, woman*'—and the woman did fill it up.

'I drink to you,' said Trumper, tossing off a quantity with the most perfect ease.

'Mild as milk,' observed he, smacking his lips as he put down the glass . . .

Toasting having begun, went on briskly, and then singing commenced. The songs were various, but all in honour of the hare. The one that gave most satisfaction had for a chorus—

> 'There's nothing can compare
> To hunting of the hare,'

which they kept hammering away at . . . Suffice it to say that our friend Scott felt the fumes of the spirit for three whole days after, and the ghost of—

> 'There's NOTHING CAN compare
> To hunting of the hare'—

haunts him still.

Hawbuck Grange, Chapter 2

No one, not even Dickens, could rival Surtees when he set himself to describe such a scene. But, after this opening, the book falls sadly away into a jumble of inconsistencies. At times Surtees seems to forget he is telling the story of Tom Scott at all. His prejudices against country inns are aired once more, there is the snarling portrayal of a bad militia regiment, his old friend Baron Gablenz of Brighton days is dragged in as the Prince of Spankerhausen and there is the usual spattering of misquotations. Surtees also uses the book as a stick to beat his critics:

'What queer books you write!' observed our excellent but rather matter-of-fact friend Sylvanus Bluff, the other day . . . 'I buy all your books,' added he with a solemn shake of his head, as though we were beggaring him . . . 'But I don't *understand* them. I don't see the *wit* of them. *I* don't see the *use* of them. *I* wonder you don't write something useful . . . I should say now you would be quite equal to writing a dictionary, or a book upon draining, and those would be really useful book works, and your friends would get something for their money.'

Gentle reader! we plead guilty to the charge of writing most egregious nonsense. Nay, we are sometimes . . . lost in utter bewilder-

ment that there should be good, honest, sane, nay sensible folks, not only idle enough to read it, but, oh wonder! of all wonders! extravagant enough to part with their good current coin to buy it!
Hawbuck Grange, Chapter 15

The closing chapters of a novel were hardly the place for this sort of reflection, and the outburst only goes to show Surtees's touchiness and readiness to let fly. Astonishingly enough, he had great hopes for *Hawbuck Grange.* As Acker-mann was not in the market he resolved to try Colburn once more, writing to him in tones which he would certainly have deplored had Nimrod used them: 'I have an offer to run it through a magazine,' he said, 'but have no objection to treat for it "first-hand" as it were. You know my style and I think my subject will admit of as good as anything I have done'.[7]

Colburn, however, had had his fingers burnt with *Handley Cross* and *Hillingdon Hall,* and was not disposed to undertake the venture. Finally Surtees persuaded Longman to accept it and it came out under the imprint of Longman, Brown, Green and Longmans in 1847 with eight uncoloured plates by Phiz. But nothing would make it sell. Three years later, with most of his stock still on his hands, Longman wrote to Surtees that the sales were 'small by degrees and beautifully(?) less. It is a pity the public do not know what amusement they might have had for 12s'. Eventually the unbound copies were sold off by auction fetching only 1s. 10d. each.

Surtees had no one but himself to blame for the failure of *Hawbuck Grange.* The plague of amateurism had him in its grip; he took far too little care over it and its merits were insufficient to overcome both its own defects and its divergence from the tastes of the day. That he was, moreover, conscious of all this is shown by his outburst concerning Sylvanus Bluff. But one of his strengths as well as his weaknesses was that he was his own man; he would go his own way; criticism while it might touch him on the raw, would never deflect him, and this in the end was to lead him to success. But, just then, he was writing too much, too quickly, and too carelessly. He was still continuing his journalism, much of which gives the impression of being dashed off with little application and no revision. He was under other pressures, too, for in addition to the considerable farming and other family cares he was becoming more and more entangled in the tortuous concerns of local politics.

Once Peel's bill repealing the Corn Laws had passed Parliament, with his usual realism Surtees accepted that nothing further was to be gained by continuing the fight against it and the only course for a practical farmer to take was to try to find a way of profiting from a situation there was no avoiding. Moreover, privately he appears to have decided that sensible pragmatism was the best course and that the attitude to adopt was one of supporting the ministry, thus gaining whatever assistance was to be obtained from its good offices. Having taken this decision he considered that he should in all honesty withdraw from the Conservative Association and wrote to a friend to say so. But he also felt that he could not publicly disown the Conservative candidates at the coming election. He himself, despite another request, declined to stand. His feelings and his motives in the whole matter were mixed. As a pragmatist, he felt that to oppose the Whig party now would be a retrograde step, but as a lifelong Conservative he could not openly say so. Once again, as had happened when he retired from the election, he sought refuge in retreat, feeling that in view of his present convictions no other course was open to him. He explained his position in a letter to the leader of the Conservative interest: 'I am so disgusted with politics both local and general, that it is not my intention to take a prominent part in the affairs of the representation; but if I can do anything for you in a quiet way I shall be most happy.'[8]

On top of all these preoccupations Ackermann wrote asking him to edit a new edition of Nimrod's *Life of Mytton* for which public demand was calling. Knowing Surtees's all-too-often expressed distaste for both Nimrod and his work it was a strange choice for Ackermann to make, and it was even more surprising that Surtees should have accepted it.

Indeed during the controversy over the inadequate proof-reading in the *New Sporting* and Nimrod's letters to *Bell's Life* which had brought down Surtees's wrath upon him, Surtees had written: 'As to the *Life of Mytton,* we just hold the same opinion respecting it that we have always done,—viz, that Nimrod would have shown himself a sincerer friend both to the unfortunate gentleman and his family, if he had suffered his eccentricities to be buried in the grave.'[9] Yet here he was, now, a few years later, accepting the task of perpetuating these eccentricities. Indeed he went even further.

Nimrod's papers were put at his disposal and amongst them he found certain anecdotes of Mytton supplied by correspondents which Nimrod had rejected as 'Very bad, very low, very improbable'. Surtees's standards were not so strict and he had no such scruples. He would, he wrote to Ackermann, 'weave in as many anecdotes as you like for £20. It is no use stinting the public for quantity and Nimrod rejected some which were quite as probable as many he admitted. He was too fastidious—always seemed to be writing "on his oath" if you understand me'.[10]

This, to say the least, accorded ill with his previously expressed opinion that the work should not have been undertaken at all. Controversialists have at times a way of contradicting themselves and Surtees, it appears, was no exception; there was one law for others and another for himself.

The work when it was published contained both Surtees's memoir and obituary of Nimrod. It equalled the success of the original edition. But it would have been more rewarding both for himself and posterity had he concentrated on his own work. It was to be two years before he published another book. When he did it was to be his breakthrough, his masterpiece, and the best sporting novel ever written in that or any other century.

CHAPTER NINE

Mr Sponge's Sporting Tour

MR SPONGE—'Soapey' to his intimates—was no hero. He was a rogue and a rascal; where horses or horse-dealing or other people's hospitality were concerned he had no morals at all, and the rudimentary polish he had acquired during ten years of living on his wits only thinly covered his many social deficiencies. His reading was confined to 'Mogg's Cab Fares' which he had always by him to while away his few idle hours. His occupation, apart from horse-dealing and fortune-hunting on horseback was 'hunting all the winter, and ... talking about it all the summer'. In a sentence, according to Surtees, 'he wished to be a gentleman without knowing how', and 'his dexterity in getting into people's houses was only equalled by the difficulty of getting him out again'.[1] That, in short, is what the book is all about and it is a measure of Surtees's achievement to have made him likeable and someone with whose self-imposed predicaments the reader sympathizes at the same time as he laughs. In addition in this book Surtees so far relented towards the hard-riding brigade as to make Mr Sponge one of them. 'He was a dauntless horseman. What man dared he dared. He would be first or nowhere.'

From the moment we meet him, 'mizzling along Oxford Street, wending his way to the West' where he proposed to visit a Mr Buckram, a horse-dealer, with a view 'to job a couple of plausible-looking horses, with the option of buying them, provided he ... could sell them for more than he would have to give Mr Buckram, exclusive of the hire', Mr Sponge is pure delight, and his encounters with the hard-riding, hard-swearing Earl of Scamperdale and his rough-rider, Field

Master, toady, and general hanger-on, Jack Spraggon, form the core of the book.

Scamperdale and Spraggon are themselves wonderful comic creations. Scamperdale was said (probably inaccurately) to be a caricature of the Earl of Wemyss, Lord Elcho's father, who had once roundly sworn at Surtees out hunting. The two cronies occupy the servants' quarters of the family mansion, Woodmansterne, where they live like tramps, eating mostly 'tripe twice-a-week—boiled one day, fried another', which they wash down with great bumpers of gin. Their only passion in life is their pack of hounds, the Flat Hat Hunt, and the sport they show, and Scamperdale is greatly afraid that Sponge, who has been through hounds twice on one of his dreadful screws, will ruin both. Their talent for invective is notable:

'Oh you pestilential son of a pontry-maid!' screeched his lordship, as Brilliant ran yelping away from under Sponge's horse's feet. '*Sing out Jack! sing out!*' gasped his lordship again.

'Oh, you scandalous, hypocritical, rusty-booted, numb-handed son of a puffing corn-cutter, why don't you turn your attention to feeding hens, cultivating cabbages, or making pantaloons for small folk instead of killing hounds in this wholesale way?' roared Jack....

'Oh, you unsightly, sanctified, idolatrous, Bagnigge-Wells coppersmith, you think because I'm a lord, and can't swear or use coarse language, that you may do what you like; rot you, sir, I'll present you with a testimonial! I'll settle a hundred a-year upon you if you'll quit the country. *By the powers,* they're away again!'...

'All jealousy,' said Sponge, spurring his horse. 'Never saw such a jealous set of dogs in my life.'

Mr Sponge's Sporting Tour, Chapter 23

Altogether it was not surprising that Thackeray wrote to Surtees to congratulate him: 'they are capital, and the Flat Hats delightful...and Scamperdale's character perfectly odious and admirable.'[2]

In addition to those two, there is a splendid gallery of subsidiary characters: the pretentious snob, Jawleyford, upon whom Sponge foists himself, and whose daughters have designs upon him; Jogglebury Crowdey with his gibbey sticks (Surtees's old schoolmaster redivivus); the dissolute Sir Harry Scattercash of Nonsuch House, 'a tall, wan, pale young man, with a strong tendency to *delirium tremens*'; and Facey Romford, too, makes a brief first appearance, the only man in the book to get the better of Sponge.

Best of all, however, for the first time Surtees gave his readers—admittedly rather late in the book—a charming, feminine, and wholly delightful heroine in Lucy Glitters. The fictional Lucy is introduced as 'the beautiful and tolerably virtuous Miss Glitters, of the Astley's Royal Amphitheatre, who had come down to spend a few days with her old friend, Lady Scattercash'.[3]

No one knows what faint stirrings of tenderness in Surtees inspired him to create her. It has been said that she was founded on the famous Skittles, mistress of Wilfred Scawen Blunt and Lord Hartington amongst others, who led the Shire fields such a merry dance in her day, but this is manifestly absurd for Skittles would have been only thirteen years old when the book was written. A more likely attribution is Miss Phoebe Higgs, one of the few hunting ladies of the day to combine grace, charm, and the ability to go well to hounds, and whom Surtees would have met when hunting with Squire Forester's pack.

Wherever she came from Lucy was indeed a charmer, and no wonder Mr Sponge was bowled over by her. She could ride, too, for both she and her friend Lady Scattercash 'used to do scenes in the circle (two horses and a flag),' and when Sir Harry's hounds ran away from their feeble huntsman she followed Mr Sponge over the park railings leaving the Courtesy Captains, the Seedeybucks, Mr Orlando Bugles, and the rest of the raffish crew that inhabited Nonsuch House well and truly pounded in their wake. Together the two of them ride out a great hunt towards the end of which Mr Sponge, seeing her taking on a water-race with a very stiff fence on the landing side and sailing over it 'like a swallow on a summer's eve', was so far moved as to exclaim: 'Well done! *you're a trump!*' It was the rarest accolade that spare-spoken man could confer, especially when his hounds were hard on their fox. And when he presented her with the brush,

he adjusted it becomingly in her hat, looking at her bewitching eyes, her lovely face, and feeling the sweet fragrance of her breath, a something shot through Mr Sponge's pull-devil, pull-baker coat, his corduroy waistcoat, his Eureka shirt, Angola vest, and penetrated the very cockles of his heart. He gave her such a series of smacking kisses as startled her horse and astonished a poacher who happened to be hid in the adjoining hedge.

Mr Sponge's Sporting Tour, Chapter 65

From the very outset the touch is surer, the pace is faster, and the storyline more coherent than in any of the other works. There is a joyousness about the whole book alien so far to Surtees's work and this despite the semi-tragic, semi-comic conclusion. For the book ends with a description of the 'Grand Aristocratic Steeple-chase' which allows Surtees to give vent to all his loathing of racing in general and steeplechasing in particular. Lucy is in tears for Sponge's safety before and during the race and sobbing with relief when he wins; Jack Spraggon meets his death when he comes down at the wall and Lord Scamperdale weeps over him while, with a typical Surteesian touch, thimble-riggers relieve both him and Jack of their watches. But 'when a lord is in distress, consolation is never long in coming' and Jawleyford, the snob supreme, duly snares him for one of his daughters. Sponge, who wins the race, would have been better off because of a crooked deal he has made, had he lost it. This does not deter him, however, from marrying Lucy and setting up a 'splendid establishment' in Jermyn Street under the name and style of SPONGE CIGAR AND BETTING ROOMS, where he advertises that he has '£116,300 to lend at three-and-a-half per cent'.

When he had finished the book Surtees appears to have had an attack of conscience at having made a hero out of such a rogue and it has been suggested that his family chided him about it. In any event, for whatever reason he added a preface to the book in the nature of an apologia:

The author gladly avails himself of the convenience of a Preface for stating, that it will be seen at the close of the work why he makes such a characterless character as Mr Sponge the hero of his tale.

He will be glad if it serves to put the rising generation on their guard against specious, promiscuous acquaintance, and trains them on to the noble sport of hunting, to the exclusion of its mercenary, illegitimate off-shoots.

The chief of these 'mercenary off-shoots' was, of course, steeplechasing. There was no governing body at that time, and malpractices proliferated. 'Steeplechases', he said,

are generally crude, ill-arranged things. Few sportsmen will act as stewards a second time . . . it is just [the] mixture of two sports that spoils both; steeplechasing being neither hunting nor racing. It has not the wild excitement of the one, nor the accurate calculating qualities of the other. The very horses have a peculiar air about them—neither hunters nor hacks, nor yet exactly racehorses. . . .

We know of no more humiliating sight than misshapen gentlemen playing at jockeys. Playing at soldiers is bad enough, but playing at jockeys is infinitely worse—above all, playing at steeplechase jockeys, combining, as they generally do, all the worst features of the hunting-field and racecourse . . .

Mr Sponge's Sporting Tour, Chapter 71

On another occasion he went on to demonstrate what a farce these 'Grand Aristocratic' steeplechases were in that grooms and valets were put up to ride under ludicrously invented foreign ranks and titles such as 'Captain de Roseville' and others, which were held to give them sufficient aristocratic qualification to go to scale, in a race supposedly confined to gentlemen riders.

The ruse by which Sponge and Buckram try to fix the race in *Mr Sponge's Sporting Tour* was not an uncommon one, nor was it usually so unsuccessful as it is in the 'Grand Aristocratic'. By and large his indictment of steeplechasing at the time it was written was fair and accurate. It was then a rascally business, unsupervised and uncontrolled and open to every sort of vice and villainy. Later public and sporting opinion forced its followers and enthusiasts to put their house in order by the formation of a governing body to be known as the Grand National Hunt Committee, and Surtees's voice may well have had some influence in bringing about this much-needed reform.

For the moment, however, Surtees was concerned with getting his story into print. In this he encountered some difficulty for his previous failures did not encourage publishers to underwrite him again. The serial market, too, was scarcely more promising for the *Sporting Review,* the old *Sporting Magazine,* and the *New Sporting* had been the subjects of a complicated series of takeovers and amalgamations, and Surtees had not for some years been on speaking terms with any of their editors.

Surtees's friend, Harrison Ainsworth had, however, just taken over the editorship of a magazine called the *New Monthly* which he had purchased from Henry Colburn in 1845. The *New Monthly* had a far wider circulation than a purely sporting one and was highly regarded in literary and social circles. Ainsworth, moreover, was a man of eclectic tastes and cast his net wide for contributors on any subject as long as they showed a mastery of it and sufficient literary ability to satisfy his critical and discerning eye. He was, too, as we have seen, a horseman himself.

Ainsworth read *Sponge* and liked it so much that he made an immediate offer for serial publication. The offer was accepted and serialization began in January 1849. The serialization was successful and the story attracted considerable attention. Ainsworth was delighted with it and he encouraged Surtees to seek publication in volume form. 'I have no doubt whatever of the success of the story', he wrote, 'when brought out with illustrations. It is unquestionably the best sporting tale ever written and beats Nimrod all to sticks.'[4]

This last sentence was a tribute which must have indeed pleased Surtees. Heeding Ainsworth's advice he at once set about finding an illustrator before looking once more for a publisher. His first choice, oddly enough, fell upon W. M. Thackeray. As a young man Thackeray had trained as an artist in Paris under George Cruikshank and some of his early drawings had appeared in *Punch*; he had also illustrated the first edition of *Vanity Fair*. But his talents as an artist were minor at best and could in no way compare with those he displayed as a novelist. *Vanity Fair* had appeared the year before; Thackeray was then at the height of his fame and one can only speculate on Surtees's reasons for approaching him as an illustrator, especially since his former illustrators were still in the field. It may have been that he thought some of Thackeray's *réclame* would rub off on to his book were he to illustrate it or, more probably, because he knew that Thackeray was sympathetic to his work. Thackeray, however, was aware of his own limitations as an artist and wrote in reply:

13 YOUNG STREET, KENSINGTON.

MY DEAR SIR,—I was very much flattered by your proposal to illustrate your tale, but I only draw for my own books, and indeed am not strong enough as an artist to make designs for anyone else's stories. You would find my pictures anything but comical, and I have not the slightest idea how to draw a horse, a dog, or a sporting scene of any sort. My friend Leech, I should think, would be your man—he is of a sporting turn, and to my mind draws a horse excellently. . . . Mr Jorrocks has long been a dear friend of mine. I stole from him years ago, having to describe a hunting scene with which I was quite unfamiliar, and I lived in Great Coram Street once too . . .[5]

Although he did not immediately approach Leech, Surtees did eventually act on the suggestion and it is to Thackeray that the credit for bringing the two men together belongs. For the moment, however, Surtees was more concerned with finding a publisher, and in this search he was meeting with little success.

First he turned to Ackermann who, however, discouraged by previous failures, wrote back, 'I am afraid of venturing on

"Mr Sponge" without I see my way clearly. The "Analysis" and "Notitia Venatica"* have damped my energies. In fact the times have so altered that we cannot tell what will take.' Next he approached Longman who also declined to venture and he, too, referred in his letter of rejection to earlier disappointments, and in it echoed many a publisher's lament then and down the ages: 'If the public had proper discrimination,' were his words, 'so many copies of "Hawbuck Grange" would not remain on our shelves . . .'

Eventually Bradbury and Evans, the publishers of *Punch* with whose editor Mark Lemon Surtees was still on terms of close friendship, agreed to bring the book out in monthly parts provided Leech would consent to illustrate it. Lemon and Leech were also firm friends, so that Lemon was able to arrange a meeting in London between Leech and Surtees. The two men immediately took to each other, a partnership was agreed upon, and the contract with Bradbury and Evans confirmed and signed.

In John Leech Surtees had found the perfect collaborator and illustrator. Although it is too much to say—as has been claimed—that Leech's illustrations 'made' Surtees's books it is at least no coincidence that the book in which they first appeared was the first of Surtees's works to command success.

A Londoner born and bred, educated, like Thackeray, at Charterhouse where they formed a lifelong friendship, Leech was originally destined for the medical profession. Like his author however, who had 'a taste for scribbling' which made the law antipathetic to him, Leech had 'a taste for drawing' which he exercised from an early age and which gave him little liking for his chosen profession. At the age of twenty-one there was some sort of financial crisis in the Leech family and Leech with relief threw up his studies to devote all his time to the precarious profession of free-lance illustrating which he hoped would enable him better to contribute to their support.

After early struggles success began to come his way. With

* *Notitia Venatica* by Robert T. Vyner (1847).

the help and sponsorship of Thackeray he became established on *Punch* as a more or less permanent contributor and with that his name was made. Aided by introductions from Thackeray he became a member of exclusive literary and sporting sets. He formed a close friendship with Charles Dickens which remained unbroken until Leech's early death and, despite failing in his application to illustrate *Pickwick* after Seymour's suicide, he did illustrate *A Christmas Carol*. He shot in Scotland with Sir John Millais, hunted in the home counties with Tenniel and Trollope, and shared a stable in Hertfordshire with Mark Lemon.

As a follower of hounds Leech was a man after Surtees's heart. William Powell Frith, Royal Academician and Victorian painter and illustrator on a grandiose scale, who was a close friend and Leech's biographer, recorded of him: 'He was a timid rider who much preferred an open gate to a thickset hedge and the high road to either.'[6] His letters to his friend Charles Adams, a country squire who mounted him and Lemon and looked for horses for them, are full of such admonitions as *'But, mind,* I won't have a beast that pulls or bolts, or any nonsense of the kind. I come out for pleasure and not to be worried. . . . I am longing to see you and have a ride across country with you. Do you think I could have the horse Mark Lemon had when he was down at Barkway? Or if I couldn't have that one, do you know of any other that would be equally TEMPERATE and WELL-BEHAVED? I have no horse at present. The last I had came down: and I am rather particular in consequence . . .'[7] Nevertheless his enthusiasm for the sport was genuine and unbounded, which would have appealed to Surtees. 'How about the hunting?' he wrote to Adams from London. 'I am continually tormented here by noble sportsmen going past my window in full fig.' That enthusiasm and the fact that he came out, in Surtees's own words, 'to amuse himself and not to astonish the others' gave him opportunities for observing his fellows in the field which he put to good use in his drawings. Like Surtees he had outstanding powers of observation and recall. The manner in which he could bring to life in his pictures each and every one of the many types that thronged the hunting fields of his day, and render them subtly or broadly comic as he wished, has a touch of genius about it. Despite the fact, too, that he appears never to have had a drawing lesson in his life and certainly never studied anatomy as did Stubbs and Landseer, he could draw horses very well, especially in action. The criticism has been made of him that all his horses are screws and there is some truth in it, but even this made him all the better as an illustrator for Surtees since almost all the horses of character appearing in his books, with the possible exception of those that carried the Earl of Scamperdale, Jack Spraggon, and Mr Jovey Jessop, were themselves screws of the utmost unsoundness and malignity. Mr Jorrocks's mounts Xerxes and Arterxerxes—so-called, it may be remembered, ''cause as 'ow ven I drives two as I'm doin' today, [Xerxes] goes leader, and in course the brown, which I call Arter-Xerxes, come arter him!'—would scarcely have passed the vet. As for Mr Sponge's Multum in Parvo, which got the better of even him at times, and Hercules (pronounced by the fancy as 'Ercles'), they were indeed very paragons among screws.

But, best of all, Leech was in character a kindly, gentle man (when, as a student, he joined a group proposing to dress up as musicians to earn some badly needed cash, they complained that do what they could they could not make him look 'really tough'), and in his drawings he softened some of Surtees's astringency and satire. 'He changed caricature into character', Dickens said of him when comparing him to Rowlandson and other cartoonists and caricaturists of an earlier generation, and Frith, perceiving and understanding this, drew attention in his *Life* of Leech to the picture of Lucy and Soapey before the 'Grand Aristocratic': 'Nothing, it seems to me, could surpass the figure of Lucy, whose expression of living fear for the safety of the bold Sponge is shown to us in one of the prettiest faces conceivable. Sponge himself is no less success-fully rendered as he smiles reassuringly at his beloved...'

The two men worked in the closest association, constantly

138

corresponding with each other over matters of colouring and details of dress and hunting accoutrements. Although Leech in his gentle and accommodating way was always ready to defer to Surtees, it is nevertheless a tribute to both men that the firm friendship and working collaboration then formed was never broken. Surtees remained an admirer of Leech to the end and, pernickety as he was about details of his characters' dress down to the last button on a coat or spur-strap on a boot, he never had occasion to find fault with Leech's rendering of their appearance, either in the hunting-field, at a ball, or in the dining salons of the great and would-be great.

The first monthly part of *Mr Sponge,* embellished with Leech's illustrations, immediately sold out its printing of 5,000 copies. The second part did a little less well, selling 4,500; the third part increased the sale to 5,500 and the remaining parts all sold over 6,000 copies each. It was a success and its further sales in volume form were assured. After years of struggle and falling sales Surtees had finally arrived on the literary scene.

But not all voices were raised in acclaim. Trollope, a hunting man and hard rider himself, is said to have disliked it; W. H. Horlock, MFH, who wrote under the name of 'Scrutator' and whose ponderous writings, justly forgotten now, had some influence in their day, came out strongly against it. There was a scathing and highly critical review in the *New Sporting* which ran to three pages of unrelieved polemic, the tone of which can be gathered from the following:

A sporting novel without a sportsman to be found in it is, at any rate, a novelty. Mr Sponge's tour has this recommendation . . . The author of Soapey Sponge, as we take it, has had a tolerable share of experience of men, women, hounds and horses, but he does not seem to think much the better of them for it. . . . Every man who asks you to his house has a daughter to hang on to you—any one who offers you a cigar, a screw to sell you. . . . Nimrod drew the sporting life of England, scene for scene, from *the life,* with the taste of a gentleman and the feeling of a sportsman. Mr Surtees, with almost as great experience and opportunity, prefers to trace out and over-colour a panorama that can give but little idea of a real sportsman's pleasures, or even of his vicissitudes.[8]

In certain circles, and not only sporting ones, the book's general tone was deprecated. Lucy, after all, was no better than she should be—did not a child, peering in one of the windows of Nonsuch House, inform her that he had been forbidden by his family to enter because 'the house was full of trumpets'! Sponge was a rogue of the first order; the Earl of Scamperdale, who had adopted Jack Spraggon ('Never was such a fine natural blackguard') as his closest friend, was held to be letting down the high standards of the aristocracy.

These criticisms appear to have affected Surtees. He was then spending a considerable amount of his time in winter hunting with Lord Elcho's hounds, staying with their Master, and indeed looking after the establishment himself when the Master was absent. He wished to dedicate the book to his friend but he appears to have been worried about his reaction to its contents, for in his letter requesting permission for the dedication he repeated what he later said in the preface: 'You will perhaps be surprised at my making such a characterless character as Mr Sponge the hero'; and went on to give an astonishing and quite inaccurate description of the nature of the book itself: 'but the fact is the work was written to decry the steeplechase, betting-list system, and winds up with one of these sorry exhibitions. The modesty of "Mr Sponge" is borrowed from a certain free and easy acquaintance of ours . . .'[9]

But neither criticism nor disapproval could stop the success of *Mr Sponge*. It attained the distinction of an American edition a few years later and, finally, long afterwards, was translated into French under the title *La Tournée Sportive de Mr Sponge*. * While he was enjoying it all Surtees was hard at work on a new book as well as cramming other multitudinous activities into a busy life.

* This translation may possibly have been initiated by André Maurois who had been introduced to Surtees's works by the second-in-command of his regiment, with whom he was serving as interpreter during the First World War and who was of the opinion that no one could understand the English until he had read *Mr Sponge*. '"I detest Dickens," said the major. . . . "No, if you wish to know the *chef-d'oeuvre* of English novels read *Jorrocks*."' (*The Silence of Colonel Bramble,* ch. 14.)

CHAPTER TEN

Young Tom Hall

ALTHOUGH as a family the Surteeses aged early and died young, at the age of nearly fifty Surtees's mental and physical energies showed no signs of flagging. His farming enterprises were as extensive as ever and, having been elected president of the Derwent and Shotley Bridge Agricultural Society he had much to do not only with his own but with his neighbours' agricultural pursuits. Never afraid to take an unpopular line, in his presidential address to the Society that year he told them bluntly that 'they were just as likely to get the moon as "their old friend protection"' back again. This remark evoked cries of 'No, no', hisses and boos and noisy interruptions. Unperturbed by these he went on to counsel his audience to drain their lands and to look to cattle for their profits rather than to corn—'plough less and pasture more'. It was eminently sensible advice even if the conservative farmers of County Durham took neither it nor him to their hearts.

But he rendered the farming community a more tangible service and gained its admiration and thanks for the manner in which he dealt with what almost amounted to a plague of mad dogs that was threatening the area. These dogs were roving uncontrolled over farms and destroying stock. Matters came to a climax when a child bitten by one of them died of hydrophobia. Surtees appealed to the Home Office for help or at least for directions as to how best these predators should be dealt with. Receiving no advice he resolved to take matters into his own hands. As a magistrate he ordered the police to apprehend all stray dogs and destroy them. This was done, there were no repercussions from his high-handed but necessary action, and the scourge ceased.

But on the question of protection which was still causing worry and discontent amongst farmers, he was adamant. It had gone never to return, and those who campaigned for its reintroduction were whistling in the wind. When appealed to to attend a meeting advocating its recall he replied in one of his terse notes, 'Dear Sir,—No more agitation for Yours very truly, R.S. Surtees.'

As well as hunting with Lord Elcho in the winter and helping to run the kennels, Surtees was paying frequent visits to London and increasing his acquaintances in literary circles. Apparently he never met either Dickens or Trollope, but the friendship with Thackeray ripened. The two men shared a legal background which both had equally detested. 'The lawyer's preparatory education is certainly one of the most cold-blooded, prejudiced pieces of invention that ever man was slave to', Thackeray wrote to a friend, and he had abandoned the law as soon as he had come of age. Of sporting tastes himself, he had lived a reckless life at Cambridge and gone down without a degree, and when he went to Paris to study he devoted himself to 'cards, dice, women, gambling and whoring'. With his patrimony gone and soon lacking the means to satisfy those tastes, in his early satiric writings he loved to puncture the pretensions of wealth and nobility. The success of *Vanity Fair,* however, changed all that for with it came introductions into society and the means to avail himself of them. He earned the reputation amongst his fellow writers of being a sycophant and wishing to mix only with men of power and position. The 'gentlemanly classes' as he called them, and the world of sportsmen of standing attracted him more than that of writers and artists. But a liking for the *louche* never quite left him. It was natural that he should be drawn to Surtees, a sportsman, a squire, and an author with an eye for the outrageous and an edge to his pen.

Surtees for his part could not but have been flattered by the attention and admiration given him by one of the leading writers of the day, for Thackeray had on occasion publicly stated that the gift of Surtees he most envied was his power of depicting character. They kept up their correspondence when they were out of London; Surtees sent Thackeray presents of grouse and peaches in season and they exchanged inscribed copies of each other's books. Thackeray was invited to Hamsterley, they met and dined together when they could in London, and exchanged sporting and literary gossip. Basically a man of kindliness, sensibility, and taste, Thackeray appears to have been one of the few men with whom Surtees could feel thoroughly at home, and with whom he could relax and ease his solitary spirit in discussion of subjects congenial to them both.

Another with whom he kept up friendship was Mark Lemon, editor of *Punch*, who very nearly brought Dickens to Hamsterley on one of their theatrical tours of the North, and it was to Lemon that he offered the first part of his new book *Young Tom Hall* with a view to serialization. The reason he did not first offer it to Ainsworth who had done so well with *Mr Sponge* is not clear, though Lemon was in high favour at the time for he had written to Surtees, 'I must congratulate you on "Mr S's" popularity. I hope your next hero will make 10,000 friends.'[1] Surtees, too, seems to have thought that the *New Monthly* was too highly priced and perhaps above the heads of the sporting public. 'The sporting world is altogether different from the general world of literature, a book serving many sportsmen for a long time,' he wrote to Leech, expressing a sentiment as true then as it is today. 'Some indeed get on capitally without any.'[2] *Punch,* too, with its light, humorous approach, its accent on sport in general and hunting in particular imported into it by Leech in his 'Mr Briggs' series, must have seemed admirably suited to his purpose.

At all events it was to Lemon that the early chapters of *Young Tom Hall* went and Lemon liked them, so much so that he went to the extent of having them set up in proof. When he read the next submissions, however, he confessed himself 'sorely perplexed' and suggested that the book be cut down. Surprisingly Surtees did not take offence at this and agreed to make the attempt, but in the end Lemon came to the conclusion it would not do for *Punch* and rejected it. He must have managed this very tactfully since no breach in their friendship resulted. Surtees then tried to interest Bradbury and Evans in bringing the book out in monthly parts but this came to nothing also. As a result, or so it seems, he turned again to Ainsworth.

In his letter of submission to Ainsworth he still appears to be smarting under the criticisms of *Sponge* for its 'low tone', or suffering from conscience about it, for he describes his hero as 'A good-natured goose without the drawback of Sponge's rascality ... Sponge who, though a good rider was a great rogue ... [He] is quite different to Mr Sponge, inasmuch as Tom has plenty of money and is a victim instead of a shark ...'[3]

Surtees was wrong in thinking that *Young Tom Hall* would redeem the impression given by *Mr Sponge* for Young Tom, the son of a provincial banker determined to make him a gentleman, so far from being the 'fine character' Surtees wanted him to be is, in fact, a weakling and a muff and as such wholly unable to carry the book on his shoulders. He is cheated over horses and women, done down by the scoundrels in the Heavyside Dragoons, and makes a fool of himself on horse and foot. Surtees's description of him as a 'good-natured goose' is apt enough but it is this very lack of backbone in its chief character which ruins the book. As always with Surtees, it is the 'shocking bad hats', the rogues, the rascals and those who sit loose to society who command the interest and carry the charm. There is a fine gallery of them, too—Lord Heartycheer, MFH, county grandee and seducer of women, well described by Frederick Watson as 'that dangerous old relic of the Regency'[4] with his huntsman-pimp Dicky Thorndyke, the appalling Colonel Blunt and his 'lovely horse-breaker' daughter, Angelena, who has her eye on his lordship who, in turn, has his, strictly dishonourable, eye on her. And one has to mention, among the horseflesh, that screw supreme Rumtouch, rechristened by the Colonel, Lily of the Valley as a 'more taking title' and who had been sold 'under all sorts of names—Sweetbriar, Carry-me-easy, Queen of Trumps, Heart-sease and many other confidence-inspiring titles' for 'many timid and many confident horsemen and horsewomen had thought it well to be rid of her . . .'5 These and others bring life to the pages, not the dreadful milksop of a hero whose misadventures, intended to point a moral, succeed only in fatally weakening the overall effect. Young Tom could carry neither the story nor the message. It was not perhaps entirely his fault for Surtees invariably failed when he tried to portray the good and the meek: he succeeded only with rogues and scamps.

George Orwell, who discovered Surtees late in his career and admired him, says of his best characters that they have no sense of sin, and this is true. They are what they are, worldly-wise, self-reliant, knowing, and resilient; neither remorse nor regret enter into their natures any more than sympathy or sentiment. Once Surtees left this hard-boiled world of cut-and-thrust and every man for himself he failed, and at times failed dismally.

But Ainsworth was charmed with the early chapters when he received them. 'I am delighted,' he wrote. 'They are all that can be desired. Go on in the same vein and you cannot fail to please everybody . . .'6 He also repeated his request to be allowed to publish over Surtees's name, a request that was, as always, refused.

For some time all went well but in November 1852 Ainsworth appears to have felt that the tale was going on too long. He wrote tactfully to Surtees enquiring from him how much further the serial had to run. On hearing that another six months would be required he wrote again hinting that an earlier termination might be necessary: 'Six months more of *Tom Hall* will just do and bring him to a proper and pleasant close; for though I individually could go on reading such a good story for ever and never tire, I am afraid the eternal cravers after novelty (subscribers to the magazine) might not be altogether of my opinion.'

The rift between the two men came only a month later

when Surtees's touchy nature and unforgiving spirit led to yet another literary quarrel. In the December issue of the *New Monthly,* whether by accident or design, with or without Ainsworth's knowledge, though as editor of the magazine the responsibility was his, the notice of the next instalment of *Young Tom Hall* to appear in the January issue contained an explicit announcement of the authorship of R. S. Surtees.

Surtees took immediate offence at this discarding of his cloak of anonymity. In the peremptory and domineering manner he adopted on these occasions he fired off a curt note to Ainsworth:

WILLIAM STREET, SUNDERLAND.
28th December 1852.

DEAR SIR,—I cannot permit the use you are making of my name, and must request you will immediately withdraw it from the New Monthly advertisement.—Yours truly,

R. S. SURTEES.

It is to be noted that, typically, he asked for neither explanation nor apology but demanded instant withdrawal. Unquestionably Ainsworth was, at least technically, in the wrong. He had earlier asked permission to publish over Surtees's name and this had been refused, and if he did not know of the erring insertion then he should have done. But it is hard to believe, as has been suggested, that he himself deliberately drafted the advertisement to draw attention to a flagging serial. He had, after all, scrupulously observed the author's desire for anonymity throughout all the preceding instalments. It is far more likely that the announcement was prepared by an underling and slipped through unobserved. It has to be remembered, too, that although Surtees insisted on technical anonymity he was known throughout the sporting world as the author of *Handley Cross* and *Mr Sponge.* Frequent references to him by name had appeared in print, hence an inexperienced sub-editor could easily have committed the mistake.

Had Surtees's letter been couched in more courteous and

less arrogant tones the outcome of the affair might well have been different. But, as it stood, Ainsworth was the last man to take such a communication lying down. He too had a temper and could be touchy where literary matters and his own reputation as an editor were concerned. He had once quarrelled bitterly with Thackeray for guying him in *Punch* after he had announced that one of his magazines would employ only authors 'eminent not only for talent but for high rank'. Unlike Surtees, however, his explosions of temper were brief and soon forgotten and the breach with Thackeray had been healed by an invitation to dinner. On this occasion, offended by the tone of Surtees's letter as indeed he had every right to be in view of their former friendly relations and all that he had done for *Mr Sponge,* and possibly with a view to winding up a serial which had begun to outlive its popularity, he wrote back almost equally tersely:

THE CLUB, BRIGHTON.

1st January 1853.

SIR,—I beg to enclose cheque on Coutts & Co. for £6 in payment of the present chapters of 'Tom Hall'.

I shall be glad if you will wind up the tale as soon as you conveniently can.—Your faithful Servt.,

W. HARRISON AINSWORTH.

This was a challenge Surtees could not overlook and he did not delay his answer:

5th January 1853

SIR,—I beg to acknowledge the receipt of your note and cheque for the January portion of 'Hall', which it is not my intention to continue. Yours obedtly.,

R. S. SURTEES.

By the time Ainsworth received Surtees's reply his resentment had cooled, though it is noticeable that even then he made no effort to resuscitate the serial:

THE CLUB, BRIGHTON.

6th January 1853.

SIR,—I have to acknowledge the receipt of your letter announcing your intention of discontinuing 'Tom Hall' in the Magazine. I do not think this fair to the Magazine or to me. But I have no wish that the tale should be continued.

In closing our correspondence, I must remark that the courtesy and consideration with which you have always been treated by me during your somewhat lengthened connection with the New Monthly ought in my opinion have rendered your present communication and that which preceded it less abrupt. I was very sorry that the advertisement occasioned you annoyance, but I had not the slightest idea that it could do so. On your request it was immediately withdrawn; and if this request had been made in terms consistent with our previous intercourse, I should have felt no occasion for further remark—except to express regret at any unintentional interference on my part with your other arrangements, if such was the case.—Your obedient servant,

W. HARRISON AINSWORTH.

Surtees ignored the letter and never spoke to Ainsworth again. He never completed *Young Tom Hall* and it was lost to posterity—though it was not a great loss—until Mr Cuming found the fragments and Messrs. Blackwood published them in their unfinished state, illustrated by G. D. Armour, in 1926. Surtees, too, did not discard it in its entirety for, as we shall see, he used it as a quarry for later books in which many of the characters, including the principal one, reappear under different names.

CHAPTER ELEVEN

Jorrocks Redivivus

JOHN JORROCKS had always been Surtees's favourite character. He had been bitterly disappointed by the failure of
Handley Cross when first published in book form. The success of
Mr Sponge encouraged him to think that the time had come
when a publisher might be persuaded to undertake a new
edition, and while *Young Tom Hall* was still running he set
about its republication. Colburn still held certain rights in the
book but Surtees wanted no more to do with him, and he
persuaded Bradbury and Evans to negotiate with him for a
release of those rights which he held. Bradbury and Evans
were not, however, enthusiastic about a reissue and wanted
instead a new, original work. Surtees pressed them, insisting
that *Handley Cross* was 'the best thing I have ever written'.
Colburn, glad to be shut of an enterprise which, after ten years
was still showing no profit, accepted £50 for his interest in the
book which Bradbury and Evans finally agreed to reissue.
Both publisher and author now realized that illustrations were
essential if the reprint was to have any chance of success. They
also knew that there was only one man who could do justice to
both characters and text and that that man was John Leech.
In July of 1852 Surtees, revelling in the success of *Sponge*, wrote
to Leech:

MY DEAR SIR,—As we clearly have the ball at our feet it may be well
to consider the best way of playing it. My idea is that a little exertion
will give us a monopoly of sporting literature . . . We have clearly hit
the nail on the head, and we may as well drive it right home . . .[1]

Leech delighted in Jorrocks and he caught to a nicety the
mixture of good-humoured rascality and amiable roguery

which formed such an ineluctible part of the great man's character and which no other illustrator before or since has been able to capture as he did. There is, too, a twinkle in Jorrocks's eye as he starts for the 'cut 'em down countries', enters Handley Cross clad in his 'versatio coat' or takes the stage preparatory to delivering his 'lector on 'untin'' which conveys to the reader the sheer enjoyment Surtees and his illustrator took in their creation.

Leech told his biographer how he found his model for Jorrocks. While staying with Charley Adams on a hunting visit, one Sunday in Barway church he observed Lady Louisa Clinton, the *grande dame* of the locality, coming up the aisle attended by her coachman. After handing her prayer books and other devotional works to her, the coachman, a rotund, ruddy-faced little man, took his place outside the pew. As he watched him it immediately occurred to Leech that here was the model for which he was searching. Surreptitiously taking out the sketch pads he always carried with him, he there and then drew the man, whose name was Nicholls, and whose form and figure he immortalized. It was a stroke of irony that would have delighted Jorrocks himself that from a secret sketch made in a church sprang the knowing, worldly, secular figure that enlivened the pages of *Handley Cross*.

But Leech did more than portray the characters—Pigg, Benjamin, Pomponius Ego, and the rest—he drew the countryside against which they existed. It is a strange omission in Surtees that he almost never depicted or described the country across which his characters hunted and which formed the background to their exploits. Although their dress, their horses, their houses, their drinks, and their meals, whether they ate off plate, pewter, or porcelain, are described down to the last detail, the last gulp of 'gooseberry champagne', the last bottle of bad claret produced from the cellar by a swindling butler, with very few exceptions the actual physical aspect of the countryside passed him by.

Leech remedied this deficiency; there is background and in some cases a very effective and beautiful background to most

Chapter heading by John Leech for
Mr Sponge's Sporting Tour, 1852

'Mr Sponge as he appeared in the
Best Bedroom'
John Leech illustration for *Mr Sponge's Sporting
Tour,* 1852

'Lucy Glitters showing the way'
John Leech illustration for *Mr Sponge's Sporting Tour,* 1852

'Michael Hardey'

Frontispiece by John Leech for *Handley Cross*, 1854

'Pigg in the Melon Frame'

John Leech illustration for *Handley Cross*, 1854

of the illustrations, whether in colour or in the text, and these added greatly to the appeal of the books.

Although Surtees's work would probably have survived without him there can be no question but that Leech enhanced it and increased its chances both of success and survival. In the first place he brought it into line with the fashion of the day for books of merit to carry illustrations, but, more importantly, his illustrations made for a fuller realization of character and setting. Surtees himself was one of the first to recognize his worth to him and to give tangible appreciation for it. He proposed to write into his preface to the new edition of *Handley Cross* a note drawing attention to the plates and drawings by 'The ILLUSTRIOUS Leech'. Modest as ever Leech protested. 'The *illustrious* is a leetle too strong! I feel that my modesty will not allow it to go out. It looks as if you attributed J's longevity to the illustrations which I cannot on any account admit. . . .' Surtees, however, insisted and the word remained. It was excised in some subsequent editions and then restored.

But if Leech himself did not maintain that the revival and survival of Jorrocks owed everything to him his admirers showed no such restraint. Frith in his biography recorded: 'Amongst the many books illustrated by Leech are some sporting novels, written, I think, by a Mr Surtees. . . . read them I cannot . . .'

In fact Frith was being less than candid when he asserted that he could not read Surtees. His text reveals that he had not only read the books but had studied them with close attention to enable him to point out with an artist's skilled appreciation the merits of the illustrations and to lend authority to his announcement that they contained some of his subject's finest work. Frith was then at the height of his power and influence; his judgement carried weight. After Frith came Thomas Seccombe's similarly dismissive notice in the *DNB*, and the Honourable John Fortescue, the historian of the British Army, writing in a symposium on the 1860s edited by John Drinkwater in 1932, said of Surtees: 'A great deal of his popularity is due not to himself but to John Leech, whose illustrations are really the best part of his books. . . . We may thank him for much shrewd observation of country life of his time, but, without John Leech, an incomparably greater man, he would have been long ago forgotten.' Another of Leech's biographers stresses the fact that 'gradually and unwittingly Leech's illustrations began to supersede the text'.[2]

These are facile verdicts and, like most such, they contain only a smattering of truth. Leech complemented Surtees; neither superseded nor supplanted him. Surtees's best books can easily stand on their own merits not only as social history or depictions of humorous caricatures but as illuminations of a timeless aspect of man's nature. Sporting and social historians of his stature are not negligible just because they are rare. His works have won their place not only in the affections of his contemporaries such as Thackeray and Ainsworth but of such diverse characters as William Morris, Rudyard Kipling, George Orwell, and Siegfried Sassoon. Even Virginia Woolf, not a noticeably kind critic nor one expected to be sympathetic to field sports, had a good word for him: 'They [the novels] have had their effect upon the language. This riding and tumbling, this being blown upon and rained upon and splashed from head to heels with mud, have worked themselves into the very texture of English prose.'[3]

Time was to prove Surtees's own affection for Jorrocks and his belief in his survival justified, and he worked hard at the new edition of *Handley Cross* in an effort to improve it, cutting, pruning, rewriting and importing new material. Charley Stobbs's adventure with the lunatic was entirely rewritten, the 'bazaar' episode dropped and the 'Cat and Custard Pot Day' introduced. The attacks on Nimrod remained. Unfortunately his faults were still with him and he was still too self-indulgent in ventilating his antagonisms and writing-up his enthusiasms. For the strangest of the new material which he brought in was the chapter 'William the Conqueror or the A.D.C'. This had already appeared as a separate story—and not a very good one—in *New Monthly* some short time before the falling out with Ainsworth, and it had nothing whatever to do with what little plot there is in the book. It concerns the masquerade at Handley Cross of one William Heveland, who plays no further part in the story and and who by adding the initials A.D.C. to his name persuades the gullible inhabitants that he is aide-de-camp to some great man, whereas he is in fact only the Assistant Drainage Commissioner. The whole thing is a typical example of Surtees's irresponsibility where construction is concerned and appears to have been put in only to enable him to guy the snobbery of small town spas and at the same time expatiate once more on the subject of drainage.

When the time for publication came, buoyed up by the success of *Mr Sponge* and encouraged by the confidence of Leech and Surtees, Bradbury and Evans printed 6,000 copies of the first monthly part. Their high hopes were disappointed. The first part failed to sell out and next month's order was reduced to 4,000 at which figure it remained for the rest of its run of seventeen parts. Nor did the one-volume reprint, despite the illustrations by the 'illustrious Leech', fare any better when published soon after the end of the monthly issues. The outbreak of the Crimean War may have militated against its chances but the fact remained that the public was not yet ready for Mr Jorrocks and his happy crew.

There was another reason, too. The ghost of Nimrod, as has been said, was not yet laid. The *New Sporting* once again came out with a savage attack on Surtees for his treatment of Nimrod in the Pomponius Ego episode and his other slighting references to him. That the author of this unsigned review knew all about the differences between Nimrod and Surtees is evident from what he wrote:

There are pages and scenes in 'Handley Cross' that would disgrace any man who ever held a pen. There is all the spleen and hate, nursed and fondled like the Spartan did the fox that was destroying him, until here it finds a bent. We can fancy and forgive any one damning another outright, in all the fury of his passion, and so have done with him; but we cannot fancy him who broods for years over is quarrel, and ends by libelling a dead man with all the puny spite his wretched taste can prompt him to indulge in.... Mr Surtees happens to have some dispute with Nimrod; and straightway the latter, living or dead, is pursued with all the rancour and hatred it is possible to imagine.... One can only regret that any person laying claim to the character of a sportsman and a gentleman could have shown a spirit so thoroughly mean and contemptible. It is the hoarded malice of years thrown, like the dirt it is, at the good name of a dead man...[4]

Here indeed was vitriol to match anything Surtees himself could have written and, to increase the offence, the anonymous reviewer had used Surtees's own name. There was, too, the unwarranted implication that Surtees had written as he did of a dead man which he would not have done had Nimrod been alive. Outraged, Surtees seized his pen and plunged into the fray:

MR EDITOR [he wrote], A writer in 'The Sporting Magazine' this month accuses me of 'insulting and blackguarding' the shade of 'Nimrod' in 'Handley Cross', as if I had written of a dead man what I would not have written of a living one. Permit me to inform him that 'Handley Cross' was published in 'Nimrod's' lifetime, and I have reason to believe that he read it—moreover that it was read by my lamented friend Mr Lockhart as it passed through the press who, I feel certain, would have suppressed any passage which he thought exceeded the bounds of good-humoured banter... Is it likely that Mr Lockhart, with his fine judgment and the intimacy with which he honoured me, would have counselled the publication of the work in a form which he thought capable of material improvement and which could have been made without any trouble?... In conclusion, let me inform the writer that when an author (from no improper motive) withholds his name from his works it is a breach of decorum to reveal it. But for this I would not have noticed his abuse.—Yours &c.,

The author of 'Handley Cross'.

Despite his bluster, Surtees felt it incumbent upon him to embark on a lengthy explanation in contrast to his usual curt and terse denials. This may indicate a feeling lingering in him that he had not treated Nimrod fairly and that some, at least, of the accusations could carry weight if not with him then with the public. Nor is his letter entirely convincing, for much of it is disingenuous. He indeed had 'reason to believe' that Nimrod had read the passage. Nimrod had all but issued a challenge over it, a fact which Surtees omitted to mention. His letter as it stands conveys the implication that Nimrod either approved or ignored it. In addition Surtees must have known very well that his 'lamented friend' Mr Lockhart who so honoured him with his intimacy, was the last man to reproach a lampoon on anyone, especially one who made such an obvious target as Nimrod.

The broadside so delivered did however, at least to some extent, serve its purpose for the reviewer withdrew the accusation of libelling a dead man and apologized. At the same time, concerning the use of Surtees's name, he commented: 'If we recollect aright, indeed, he has been before this identified in other publications.'[5]

Surtees's angry and involved reply may, in fact, have done the book more harm than good. Such rejoinders by authors even when followed by apologies and withdrawals are often best avoided for they can have the effect of drawing attention to and prolonging the impact of the original adverse review. Moreover in this case it may well have been damaging to bring back into public notice the old quarrel between himself and Nimrod for Nimrod's name remained one to conjure with in sporting circles. His *Life of a Sportsman* and *Life of Mytton* were still selling far better than Surtees's own works; his friends and admirers were legion and faithful. The special pleading in Surtees's letter would not have gone unnoticed and the whole affair drew attention to a side of his character and his work which were then and still remain a blemish on his virtue as a man and his standing as an author.

Worse still the review, while admitting the merits of *Handley Cross* and the authenticity of the sporting scenes and characters, had gone on to air once more the then all but universal complaint against Surtees's work, and in so doing had claimed attention for a younger author and competitor:

Even in his best moods—and we gladly admit he has many of them—the author of 'Handley Cross' takes no very high ground.... He constantly associates, moreover, as we have before had to remark, the love of the chase with the love of £.s.d. All his characters are intent on 'doing' each other.... We question, indeed, whether he [the novice] would be led to believe from them that the character was at all compatible or the amusement in accordance with the proper taste of an English gentleman. Is there no one to teach him better? Luckily we have ... If we were asked to name any work which, within the last few years, has given the best description of English society as it now is, we should unhesitatingly turn to 'Digby Grand'.... If anyone is anxious to know how an English gentleman does really occupy himself, what are his pursuits, his pleasures, his cares, we can recommend him to no better authority than 'Digby Grand'.

Digby Grand was written by George John Whyte-Melville in the Nimrod tradition of fair ladies, frank and manly heroes, and fast and flying hunts across the grass countries. A serving soldier in the Coldstream Guards, Whyte-Melville himself declared his hunting creed to be 'it's pace that gives life to the chase' which was, of course, the very antithesis of all that Surtees stood for. *Digby Grand* (in three volumes) far outsold *Handley Cross* but Whyte-Melville was one of the few to have read, liked, and appreciated Surtees's books. Whatever offence he might have committed in Surtees's eyes by his style of writing and subject matter was purged by the letter of appreciation and admiration which he wrote to him on reading the new edition of *Handley Cross*. The sentiments expressed in the letter were genuine for Whyte-Melville was yet another author to be influenced by Surtees, especially in his later work. His last, best, and most successful book, *Market Harborough,* which stands up well today, clearly shows this influence. Here, Whyte-Melville discarded the 'aristocratic' tradition and made his hero a small squire with a provincial pack visiting the fashionable countries, and used him as a medium for gentle satire on the swells of the day. But it, too, outstripped its greater progenitors in the matter of sales for, as Mr Watson wryly records, it went through seven editions in as many years while one solitary printing of *Handley Cross* sufficed to meet demand during the same period.[6] Indeed in 1858, four years after publication of the second edition, Surtees was sadly noting: 'I believe it is paying something. At all events it was out of debt last summer.'[7]

The disappointments, the adverse criticisms, the quarrel with Ainsworth coupled with the failure of the new edition of *Handley Cross,* had their effect on Surtees. A new element of savageness previously absent from his satire made its appearance in his next two books, but before they appeared Surtees was involved in a new venture, a return to journalism, which occupied him as much as his efforts over *Handley Cross.*

CHAPTER TWELVE

The Field

As he had been cast down by the failure of *Handley Cross* so Surtees's spirits had been raised by the success of *Mr Sponge*. At almost the same time as he was writing to Leech the vainglorious sentence 'We have the ball at our feet...'[1] he was contemplating a new and different undertaking brought on, it seems, by another rebuff which he took as a personal affront.

During the hunting season of 1852 he proposed to *Bell's Life* that he should carry out a hunting tour on their behalf and write a series of articles on his experiences. 'I have more horses than I can work with Lord Elcho', he wrote, 'and the rail enables me to go here, there and everywhere.'[2] *Bell's Life*, however, in the person of its editor Mr Dowling, was not disposed to accept the expense of such a venture. Dowling put forward another suggestion which Surtees considered beneath him and he turned it down. But he was not prepared to give up his idea of further sporting tours nor was he one to suffer a rebuff quietly. Immediately his thoughts turned to the founding of a new and rival sporting magazine. He first approached his old acquaintance Mr Spiers to discover whether he would undertake the printing. When he received a favourable reply he entered into negotiations with Bradbury and Evans regarding publication:

I was thinking of an eight page, sixpenny paper . . . I would make it a sporting, a landowner's, and a sort of high-life-in-London paper— with a summary of all that is going on. With regard to the racing I would not attempt to set up any wiseacre to mislead the public on these matters, experience abundantly proving that the pretended prophets know nothing about the matter. If they did they would go

158

and make their fortunes by betting instead of dabbling in ink.

The 'Nimrod' I think, will be the best title, hitting the nail on the head, in which 'Bell's Life' is notoriously weak.... There is an undoubted field for a *gentleman's* sporting paper...[3]

The choice of the name 'Nimrod' was an extraordinary one for Surtees to have made in the light of his attitude to the man and it was, in the event, the only one of his suggestions with which Bradbury and Evans were prepared to differ. The idea of a new sporting magazine appealed to them and so, with Surtees acting as adviser and general overseer, the preparations for publication went ahead. Its name was left in abeyance for a little while and then, after discussion, the title *The Field* was finally decided upon. Under that title it has survived and is still flourishing to this day; its first number appeared on 1 January 1853, with Surtees's old friend Mark Lemon in the editorial chair.

No one knows who suggested the name but it may well have been Lemon, who had great journalistic flair. Surtees was delighted with Lemon's appointment and wrote to him immediately he heard of it:

I am glad you come in for your admirable management of 'Punch' makes me sure it will be done as it ought. I should much like to talk matters over with you, and if you can't get down here I shall be in town in November, though that is the cream of the hunting season, and things ought to be arranged before. As 'Sponge' is to be completed before November, I should appear in the hunting countries with advantage, and get things forward for a start in January.[4]

From this it is clear that he was determined to embark on the hunting tours which had provided the motive for his suggestion of the new magazine. It is also worth noting once more, as the letter discloses, that, despite his furious protestations whenever his anonymity was breached by those whom he disliked or who had in some way offended him, he was not above making capital of his name when it suited his purposes.

Even Mr Cuming, the most kindly of commentators, was moved to remark of this letter, 'The secret of authorship, it will be observed, was a very open one'.[5] What Ainsworth, who was suffering persecution for revealing it at almost exactly the same time as this correspondence was taking place, would have thought—and written—had he known of it is interesting to speculate.

There can be no question, however, that the new publication was fortunate in having the benefit both of his experience in journalism and of his name, even when disguised under the attribution 'By the author of *Handley Cross* and *Mr Sponge's Sporting Tour*'. He provided Lemon with lists of those prominent in sport or society who were likely to become subscribers and he stressed to him the importance of obtaining illustrations from the leading sporting artists of the day amongst whom, naturally enough, he named Leech as the very best. Lemon well knew of Leech's over-production, overwork, and unpunctuality but he managed nevertheless to extract from him 'a capital "heading" and a large drawing for No. 1'. He also enlisted Hablot K. Browne (Phiz) who had worked with Surtees before, and a future Royal Academician, Richard Ansdell. Browne could draw animals with accuracy ('I wish I could draw a horse like Browne', Leech once said) but his creatures, human and equine, lacked the fun and fire Leech's pen put into his and which Surtees so admired. Ansdell was of the school of Landseer, indeed his paintings were and sometimes still are taken for those of his master. Surtees particularly disliked the softness and sentimentality of the style. Lemon had told him in one letter, 'Write whenever you have anything to find fault with and we will endeavour to amend' but about Surtees's criticisms of Ansdell he went on to say 'You are quite right as to the value of Leech's drawings but they are not always to be got, and you are wrong about Ansdell's. No less than six comissions for pictures have come through the "Field" office during the last five weeks.'

Lemon was correct to stress the value of a contributor who brought in commissions, for *The Field,* like most new publications, had to struggle for existence. Nor was Surtees's own optimistic prediction in his original letter that 'writers will soon tumble in when they find there is a market for them' borne out, since established authors, for some reason, were fighting shy of submitting work.

Surtees himself tried to fill the gap as he had done long ago with the 'old' and *New Sporting* magazines, writing leaders when required and submitting unsigned articles. He contemplated contributing another Jorrocks series to its pages but this in the end only ran to three letters purporting to be written by the great man himself. They show neither Surtees nor Jorrocks at his best for they are couched in Surtees's very worst vein of sham-cockney jocosity and, with the exception of the last where Jorrocks recites a litany commencing, 'Confound all farmers, I say, wot deal in double ditches', they read almost like self-parodies.

His reports of his hunting tours, too, were not an unqualified success. With a strange inconsistency in view of his former animadversions against them, his first tour took him into the very heart of the Shires. Once there, perhaps in view of his altered position in life, he was not above fawning on the mighty and the great. He was pleased and flattered by the attention shown him by the great Assheton Smith of whom he wrote, 'There is still some advantage in hunting with a former Master of the Quorn', and Sir Richard Sutton, the then Master of that pack, was praised for his intention of hunting eight days a week, the two extra days being somehow run in contemporaneously with a subsidiary pack at Market Harborough maintained by his son.

He could not, however, always stay with the great in their houses and his opinion of hotels had not changed: 'A friend of mine was charged 6s for a bad fish and mutton chop dinner in a coffee room' he wrote of one in Leamington, their charge of 30s. a week for stabling a horse, he considered outrageous and said so in no uncertain terms—10s. or 12s. at most would, he said, be ample.[6]

Methods of transport, at least, had changed for the better

and he was now a firm advocate of the railways whose 'soft luxuriance has almost obliterated the recollection of the hard old coaching times'. But he worried about what would happen if he were 'to see a gallant pack clustering on a railway, with an express train bearing down on them at the rate of forty miles an hour'. This very question was answered for him by reports in the magazine for on 12 February 1853 the Essex Hounds, hard on their fox near Witham, drove on to the rails but the guard, catching sight of the field pursuing them, stopped the train; some months later, when the Hon F. Petre's staghounds crossed the line between two approaching expresses both of them pulled up to allow the hunt to pass unharmed.

Two other leaders bear unmistakable marks of Surtees's hand. With his experiences of the plague of mad dogs in Durham fresh in his mind he protested at the refusal of the Government to act firmly in dealing with the danger of hydrophobia: 'If the Government will not strengthen the hands of the justices by giving them the power of enforcing prudent precautionary orders, it is as well that the country should know with whom the blame rests.' And once more he mounted his steeplechasing hobby-horse: 'We are no advocates of steeplechasing, we look upon it as neither fish, fowl, nor good salt herring. Indeed we think that a bunch of good salt herrings drawn at random over a hunting country, with ten or twelve couple of good hounds to hunt it, would be infinitely superior to any steeplechase that ever was arranged.'[7]

But despite all Surtees's efforts and contributions the paper did not prosper. In October 1853 Lemon wrote frankly to him and asked him to become hunting editor. Surtees wrote back:

I am sorry to hear of the unproductive state of your 'Field', which I had hoped had shared the general farming prosperity . . . my field of observation this season will be limited to a single hunt or two, and those not of the *élite* of the world.

Mr Whyte-Melville is out and out the best man of the day, being a fine sportsman and a capital writer, living in the very cream of the thing (Boughton, Northamptonshire) . . . I have been having a turn with a couple of packs near here the last two days but saw nothing worth relating save a huntsman arrive dead drunk at the meet . . .[8]

Whyte-Melville, busy with *Digby Grand,* also declined the appointment but in any event by the end of November Bradbury and Evans had disposed of their unprofitable investment. The new owner was an actor-manager of the period, a Mr B. N. Webster who succeeded in losing no less than £9,000 on the paper in the space of eleven months. Almost exactly a year later it was sold again this time to a Mr E. W. Cox who stated his intentions clearly: 'A love of the country and of rural occupations is a characteristic of Englishmen; and it is the design of *The Field* to administer to that wholesome taste. Hunting, shooting, fishing, yachting, cricket, riding and driving are the field sports which we shall embrace'.[9]

Surtees's importance to the paper diminished with the new regime and his contributions gradually fell away. He may have been glad enough of it for although in the years to come *The Field,* like his own works, was to enjoy an ever-increasing popularity and prosperity, just then it seemed doomed to failure and, besides, other preoccupations were pressing upon him.

CHAPTER THIRTEEN

Ask Mamma

DURING the year 1855 Surtees had been discussing with Leech ideas for a new sporting novel which he proposed to serialize if he could find a magazine prepared to accept it, for the quarrels with Ainsworth and various magazines had considerably restricted his market. This project, however, was temporarily put aside for at the beginning of the following year he was approached by Longman to know if he would edit a new edition of Blaine's *Encyclopaedia of Rural Sports* in which his firm held the rights.

Very unwisely in view of the demands on his time and unquestionably to the detriment of his own original work Surtees accepted the commission, though in so doing he cannot have anticipated what a monumental and time-consuming task it was to be. His motives for undertaking what was at best hack-work must forever remain obscure for he never revealed them but it is probable that, since he never wanted for money, the effect on his thin-skinned and sensitive nature of the adverse criticism the new edition of *Handley Cross* had received, combined with the lack of public response to it, played a considerable part in his decision to put off writing a new novel. In any event accept he did, and threw himself wholeheartedly into the task. His letter of acceptance sheds light on his state of mind at the time and shows the sort of detailed examination to which contributions were likely to be subjected:

Please send me down the last edition in numbers, so that I may distribute the parts among the different followers of each pursuit. Of course you know I don't put my name to anything—either my own name or a fictitious one,—but I shall not do you less justice on that account.

How would it do to get Leech to do a few hunting cuts? His name is great and good, and as this arrangement will postpone a projected serial we had arranged, I daresay he would keep his hand in by doing a few cuts for you.

I don't much like your frontispiece repeated at page 456. A rein in each hand is bad, and the whip is I don't know where. The fox at page 443 is like a hairy worm. The 'Pack Master' page 492, is evidently the huntsman. I never heard a Master of Hounds designated a 'Pack Master' before. A pack master down here means a pedlar with a pack on his back.

I should not like to be the excited gentleman at page 496 if his master caught him. Altogether I think an infusion of 'Leech' would be beneficial, and his name is as good as the lion stamp on silver. If you like I will sound him.[1]

This letter also shows how high Leech stood in his regard: 'as good as the lion stamp on silver'—coming from one as stinting with his praise as Surtees there could scarcely have been a greater compliment.

The team of authors which he picked or which Longman picked for him proved dilatory and difficult. Leech, who only undertook the work as a favour to Surtees and whose health was already beginning to suffer from overwork, was more unpunctual than ever in sending in his drawings. Unlike Lemon who frequently had to take a cab to Leech's house and sit smoking a cigar while he waited for the next *Punch* drawing to be completed, Surtees from Hamsterley could only chivvy his artist by letter, receiving in return such plaintive complaints as 'Blaine has almost worried me to fiddlestrings'.

Longman, too, protested at the delay and wondered if the enterprise would ever be ready for publication. In the end, after eighteen months hard labour it was all finished—1,230 pages with 600 illustrations by Alken, Leech, Landseer's brother Thomas, and others. It is now quite forgotten.

Apart from the *Encyclopaedia* and his other concerns,

Surtees had yet another call on his time during this period, for in 1856 he was appointed High Sheriff of the County of Durham. It was typical of his disregard for convention and dislike of show that one of his first acts in that office was to propose in his speech of welcome to the judges on circuit that in future they should be met on arrival by a carriage and pair instead of the traditional coach and four. But if he was determined to cut down show and expense in that deparment of the law he also fought hard for the rights of the new county-court judges whose proposed salary scale he considered much too low for their duties and position. Always cognisant, too, of his public responsibilities, he was mindful of the poor and oppressed who could not speak for themselves. Inspecting the workhouses of the county he was horrified by what he saw, for conditions in many of them were scandalous. Indignant at the lack of concern shown for the poor wretches consigned to them, he wrote a typically trenchant letter to *The Times:*

The workhouse is conducted under the control of a board of guardians, the great majority selected from the most noisy, vulgar and ignorant of the small tradesmen of the parish . . . Under such management, is it surprising that from time to time the public are shocked at revelations of workhouse tyranny which, in spite of all attempts to smother them, will make their cry of anguish to be heard? Is it astonishing that at one workhouse in Southwark it is an ordinary occurrence to find upwards of thirty young children, mature women, and old tramps sleeping together in the basement storey of the workhouse upon loose straw, covered with vermin, rotten with disease, and foul with every conceivable odour arising from bad legs and filthy garments?

He was, too, continuing to play an active part on the Bench; he became a leading member of the board of guardians in his parish and sought to strengthen other boards by recruiting members of his class on to them and striving to imbue them with his own sense of public duty and responsibility. On the Bench and off it he was tireless in taking up the cause of those whom he thought had been wronged, on one occasion fighting another board of guardians single-handed in the interests of a poor cottager—and winning.

It was no wonder that his new book had to be delayed and that with all these preoccupations upon him, he turned back to the unfinished *Young Tom Hall* for some of its scenes and many of its characters. This book was the project referred to in his letter to Longman, and it was Longman who finally agreed to publish it in monthly parts illustrated by Leech, having abandoned the idea of magazine serialization. The book was *Ask Mamma, or the Richest Commoner in England*—even the sub-title was borrowed from an earlier short story by Surtees written some years before and described by him as 'unsuccessful'. During its monthly run it inspired the 'Ask Mamma' polka which Surtees then incorporated into his description of the hunt ball, but it achieved little else. Longman did not undertake the publication in the end, and it appeared under the imprint of Bradbury and Evans.

Ask Mamma shows a sad falling off from *Mr Sponge* and *Handley Cross*. There is none of the gaiety which runs like lightning through the pages of those books, illuminating them with flashes of near genius. The central character is another muff, the Richest Commoner in England, another Young Tom Hall all over again. Lord Heartycheer, his huntsman Dicky Thorndyke, and the flirt, Angelena Blunt are all recreated as Lord Ladythorne, Dicky Boggledyke, and Miss de Glancey, and each of them loses something in their renascence. In place of fun there is satire, savage and unremitting. The two most telling—and most unpleasant—characters in the book are Sir Moses Mainchance and his hanger-on Cuddy Flintoff.

Cuddy Flintoff is a marvellous if merciless portrait of a type every sportsman knows to this day—the man who drinks and talks the part but never performs. Surtees describes him, and it has never been done better:

Mr Cuthbert Flintoff, commonly called Cuddy Flintoff, an 'all-

about' sportsman, who professed to be of all hunts but blindly went
to none ... He dressed the sportsman, too, most assiduously, bird's-
eye cravats, step-collared striped vests, green or Oxford-grey
cutaways, with the neatest-fitting trousers on the best bow legs that
ever were seen.

Chapter 68

Sir Moses himself sums him up when he tells Billy 'Oh, he's
only an afternoon sportsman that. He's greatest after dinner'.
Cuddy duly gets his come-uppance when he is persuaded
into a steeplechase match with Billy's allegedly French
servant Jean Rougier, otherwise Jack Rogers, and is roundly
defeated.

Sir Moses Mainchance, baronet, is a far more formidable
character. In him is typified everything Surtees detested in
human nature and in the false values of the new squires
then beginning to penetrate the old county oligarchy, and
who owed their ability to do so to money and nothing else.
Loathsome in all his aspects, his is a powerful and convincing portrait though it cannot but be regretted that in
drawing it Surtees yielded to the anti-Semitism of his time
by stressing his Jewish origin. Sir Moses's great fortune,
founded on his father's talent for usury, has been employed
by him to better himself, first by purchasing a baronetcy
and then in buying a country estate and the Mastership of
the Hit-im and Hold-im Shire Hounds. In Surtees's eyes he
can do nothing right:

In truth, if nature had not made him the meanest, Sir Moses would
have been the most liberal of mankind, for his life was a continual
struggle between the magnificence of his offers and the penury of
his performances. He was perpetually forcing favours upon people,
and then backing out when he saw that they were going to be
accepted ...

Chapter 61

He is pilloried mercilessly for his social, sporting, and racial
shortcomings. His magnificent house is furnished with
shoddy, his servants are third-class because he will not pay

for their betters—a ticket-of-leave butler, a delirium tremens footman, a 'job-cook', and a drunken huntsman. He is incapable of managing his estate or dealing with his tenants, and he is not above swindling anyone, including his house-guest, Mr Pringle, over a horse.

The 'match-making mothers and blushing virgins' as Kipling described them, are, too, there in plenty to catch 'the Richest Commoner' if they can. Billy's worldly-wise mother —who knows a thing or two about ensnaring a man and who captures Lord Ladythorne himself in the end—writes him letters of cynical counsel:

It is much easier to get entangled with a girl than to get free again . . . the stupidest woman that ever was born is better than the cleverest man in love affairs . . . *Don't be more attractive to one sister than the other* . . . Be cautious, too, about letter-writing . . . love letters are a woman's flags and banners, her trophies of success . . . the girl's mammas read them, their sisters read them, their maids read them, and ultimately, perhaps a boisterous junior barrister reads them to an exasperated jury.

Chapter 24

No one comes out well from Billy's travails and travels. Major Yammerton, Master of 'Haryers', will stick Billy with a horse or one of his daughters given half a chance. The daughters dress affectedly, their exaggerated crinolines taking up so much room in the coach carrying the party to church that the Major has to ride on the box. From this eyrie he descries his hind's daughters turned out in much the same style as his own and promptly decides to dock the man's wages by a shilling a week. 'We think the Major's remedy for reducing it [the mania for dress] by no means a bad one', is Surtees's comment on the effect his daughters' pretensions have on the unfortunate servant's standard of living. But Surtees seldom had any sympathy for servants; they were, from hunt servants downward, a race apart, mostly dirty, unreliable, and unscrupulous.

Lawyers, too, in the person of Mr Carroty Kebbell, receive

a drubbing. The scene of Angelena Blunt's discomfiture in the rainstorm and loss of Lord Heartycheer because of it which appears in *Young Tom Hall,* is repeated almost word for word in Miss de Glancey's losing of Lord Ladythorne in similar circumstances, down to the old Earl's sour remark as he pulls off his sodden boots, 'I was right—women *have* no business out hunting.'

The only softening of the satire, cruel, savage, and unrelieved, for this is a book not of humour but of savage mockery, is in the account of the saving of the hare from Major Yammerton's 'Haryers'.

It will be recalled that Surtees's sympathies as a huntsman lay with 'the timid hare' and his hopes were always for mercy to be shown her. Indeed, taking hunting as a whole, he respected the quarry more than those who pursued it. As in the case of many who possess a similar reserved, introspective, and ingoing nature it came easier for him to express compassion towards animals than towards his fellows, and here he does so: 'There she lay with her head to the air, panting and heaving and listening for her dread pursuers coming. Oh, what agony was hers! . . . And now poor puss being a little recruited steals out of her hiding place [and] so poor, weary, footsore, fur-matted puss, goes hobbling and limping up to the farm buildings as if to seek protection from man against his brother man.' The farmer's wife exclaiming 'It's that mad old major and his dogs', hides and succours the hare, foiling the pursuit, and the whole scene is enhanced by Leech's tender drawing in which poor puss at the farmyard gate can almost be seen to be pleading for mercy.[2]

Surtees would never extend such clemency to the fox who commanded neither affection nor compassion, only respect as a worthy and wily antagonist against whom to pit his wits, and who was too much of an equal to require mercy. 'There is something about that noble animal that forbids our treating him slightingly. He should be hunted like a gentleman . . .'* And there is no pity, only the salute of one master of the wild to another, in any of his many descriptions of the fox: 'A fine grey-backed old fellow, with his neat ears well laid back and a well-tagged brush, [who] crossed the ride about fifty yards higher up at an easy listening pace as if calculating the amount of scent he was leaving behind.' And did not Mr Jorrocks say 'He's a perfect symmetry and my affection for him is a perfect paradox. In the summer I loves him with all hardour of affection; not an 'air of his beautiful 'ead would I hurt but when hautumn comes, then dash my vig, 'ow I glories in the pursuing of him . . . it's not that I loves the fox less but that I loves the 'ound more . . .'

Considering that the whole human race comes out of it so badly it was not to be expected that *Ask Mamma* would be successful, nor was it; indeed a close friend of Surtees' voiced the general feeling about the book when he wrote to him, 'You are all-powerful in exposing pretence, shams, and ostentation &c.,&c., and in gathering up small traits or evidences to crush the culprits . . . There is only one defect which I should like to hint at. Why not make your satire effective by restraint? Do give us a *good* character, man or woman; honest, truthful domestic, trying to do what duty requires to God and man and happy accordingly . . .'[3]

It is just possible that this letter or others like it carried some weight. In his next book, *Plain or Ringlets?*, published

---

* Satirist as he was Surtees here laid himself open to the satire of another though it was left to A. P. Herbert nearly a hundred years later to put it into words:

> And I vow and aver
> That foxes prefer
> To be killed, as it were, in their armour
> By an aristocrat
> In a shiny top-hat
> And not by an underbred farmer.

It is worth noting, too, that a latter-day intellectual, George Lyttelton, in a letter to Sir Rupert Hart-Davis, described his encounter with a fox in words which Surtees himself might have used: 'I still recollect the piercing intelligence of his eye—all curiosity and vigilance and a general air of being equal to any occasion.'

two years later by Bradbury and Evans, although the general tone is still querulous, Surtees did include one character who reveals a certain softening of attitude. This is Jovey Jessop Esq., MFH, who can fairly be said to owe his origin to Surtees's mentor and object of youthful hero-worship, Ralph Lambton, MFH.

If Sir Moses Mainchance epitomized all that Surtees loathed and despised, Jovey Jessop characterized all that he found admirable in humanity. Master of a small establishment he hunts hounds himself at his own expense. He is 'A good fellow—a thorough sportsman, and a hearty, hospitable man ...' 'Whatever Mr Jessop did he did well' which includes 'keeping two cooks, an Englishman to cook his beefsteak for breakfast and a Frenchman to send up the fricandeau &c for dinner'. In addition Mr Jessop keeps 'some capital port, fine rich, ruby, silky wine, that connoisseurs would give any money for ...' All this is contrasted with the shoddy pretensions of the household and hunt presided over by one of Surtees's 'shocking bad' aristocrats, the Duke of Tergiversation. His Grace, who is made an object of scathing satire, has Jewish origins from which spring many of his faults, for his immediate progenitor bore the name of Duke Fortunatus Emmanuel and in Leech's drawings he is made to bear a marked resemblance to Sir Moses Mainchance.

During the writing of *Plain or Ringlets?* Surtees was once more acting as High Sheriff, standing in for his friend Sir William Clavering. He had reached his middle fifties and age was catching up with him at last. He was withdrawing ever more into himself; disappointment, as Mr Watson records from a private letter which was disclosed to him, was leaving its mark upon him, depression of the spirit, always endemic in a character such as his, was claiming him ever more often.

As a writer, invention had never been his strong point. Observation combined with total recall were the mainsprings of his talent. Now even his great energies were flagging and with that came fewer opportunities for exercising his piercing eye and probing mind upon fresh scenes and people. Thus, once again, for this new book, although he made a new nonentity, Mr Bunting, its hero, he was compelled to turn to *Young Tom Hall* as a quarry for many of its characters. Hall senior, the banker, Tom's father, with his eternal monologue 'Sivin' and four's ilivin', and eighteen is twenty-nine' becomes Jasper Goldspink, banker, always muttering an identical chant, waging an eternal war with the Duke of Tergiversation over his debts, and finally being outwitted by Johnny O'Dicey, the Irish gambler, over an acceptance on a bill. Surtees in this book went even further back in memory than *Young Tom Hall* to find his characters. Johnny O'Dicey, 'a gentleman of large in the sharxing way' is none other than the redoubtable Colonel Charrittie with whom Surtees had shared the Mastership of Hounds in Boulogne thirty years ago, and the Baron Gablenz of those far-off Brighton days is dragged in once more, this time as Prince Pirouetteza to make a fool of himself at the Duke of Tergiversation's shoot.

As a novel *Plain or Ringlets?* is negligible, though it may have value for the social historian in its pictures of a mid-Victorian watering-place, its picnics, race-meetings, and mild diversions, its reflections on the dangers of high play and *louche* society, discounting bills, railways, London clubs, old and new squires, and virtually anything else which occurred to Surtees ruminating at his standing-desk and looking back over the years.

CHAPTER FOURTEEN

Gone to Ground

WITH failure still dogging him and the high hopes raised by the success of *Mr Sponge* now seven years in the past, Surtees set about preparing his last and what many consider to be his best novel. While he was working on it he made it known that this was to be his final work of fiction; so it proved to be, but not for the reason he thought. He intended to close his writing career with his autobiography but in the event he did not live to see the publication of *Mr Facey Romford's Hounds,* and the autobiography was never completed.

As always other concerns interrupted work on the new novel. He was still exercising personal control down to the most minute detail on his farm of 250 acres at the Hagg. In addition there were 700 acres of woodland conducted as a commercial enterprise under his supervision and which he insisted must show a profit at the end of each year. His colliery interests, too, had to be given his attention. Not content with all these Surtees resolved to commit to print his thoughts and opinions on Durham farms, farmers, and farming both in general and in particular, and to combine these with his own directions on how they might be bettered or better themselves. When finished it was a long, detailed, and comprehensive treatise which included a passage on coal-mining in Durham, how it was and how it should be conducted. Although set up in proof this treatise was never published and only came to light after his death. Dealing as it does with dry and technical subjects which even then were of only local or topical interest, it might be expected to be unreadable now. But Surtees managed to stamp it with all the hallmarks of his mordant mind and trenchant style.

Much of Durham consisted of smallholdings. Surtees did not think highly of their occupiers and said so:

A small capitalless Durham farmer is, indeed, a deplorable object.... A man has been known to take a hundred and twenty acres of land whose capital consisted of two old horses and three sovereigns! That, of course, not answering, he was presently at the door, when on producing his seed bill for the next comer to pay, he was found to have seeded an eighteen acre field with sixteen shillings worth of seeds.... No wonder that a south-country landowner, after inspecting several small farms, asked if weeds formed part of the rotation of crops...

As for the women called in to work on the farms, it was not to be expected that they would escape without castigation:

Next to a Durham horse's corn, a Durham female's hours of labour are the most uncertain. They come crawling to the fields at all hours and take themselves off in a huff at the slightest provocation. A shilling a day, summer or winter, is the lowest remuneration they will accept for their services, or rather for getting up appetites for their meals...[1]

Finally, his conclusion was: 'It may seem harsh in thus abolishing the race of small, capitalless Durham farmers; but in so far as the county of Durham is concerned it is really a kindness, for experience abundantly proves that they never advance themselves.'

Altogether the treatise gives every indication of having been written in the same bitter and despairing mood which had brought forth *Ask Mamma* and *Plain or Ringlets?* And if this mood still possessed him he had some reason for it. As we now know loneliness and depression of the spirit had him more often in their grip. Becoming disinclined to face the journey to London he was seeing less of Thackeray, who was taken up with the editing of the *Cornhill,* and of his other literary friends. Lockhart was dead, he had quarrelled irretrievably with Ainsworth; Leech, too, was becoming more and more consumed by overwork; ill health and insomnia were beginning to take their toll of him, and he was even contemplating an ill-advised venture into painting in oils. Thackeray had a little earlier declined an invitation to Hamsterley, pleading pressure of work—'Lord, Lord, how the people (&c) are pouring in!'—and Leech also wrote warning Surtees not to make the journey south: 'This is not a tempting time for travelling nor do I think it would be necessary for you to leave your home to take a journey in the snow.'[2]

Hardest of all for Surtees to bear in those years was the fact that what little nerve he had for crossing the country was deserting him. Thus his greatest interest and joy in life, that of riding to hounds and watching them work, was taken from him. Refusing to give up his beloved sport he continued to ride to meets and to the end of his life, though he became ever more wary of the weather, he could be seen, mounted on an old white cob, creeping along the roads, using his unrivalled knowledge of the country and the ways and wiles of its foxes to work out the direction and destiny of hounds as they ran.

Surtees himself has left no clue why, in his new book, he abandoned the savage satire of *Ask Mamma* and *Plain or Ringlets?* and turned back to the mellowness and humour which had so inspired *Mr Sponge* and given it its appeal. It may have been an urge to find again the source where success lay and to repeat it; it may have been that for the moment at any rate those last two books had purged the contempt for everybody and everything which then possessed him. It may have been that, looking back over his life and calling on memory to aid inspiration he simply found again, as ageing men sometimes will, the flavour of youth bringing back once more to his mind and pen the rogues and rascals he had laughed at in the past together with the pretty women of the *demi-monde* he had admired and perhaps dallied with in long-ago London.

Whatever the reason, if he was seeking success he found it, for he once more got into print all the fun and the fire and the gaiety which had enlivened *Mr Sponge* and the best pages of *Handley Cross*. Once more, too, he had a hero—of sorts—in the rough and ready, hard-bitten, hard-riding Facey and a real heroine in the sweet and lovely Lucy Glitters, making her re-appearance. It is yet another paradox of his extraordinary nature that in his two most successful novels he should have had as chief characters the very type he said he most detested in the hunting field—the hard rider to hounds for Facey, as indeed he showed and Surtees said of him, 'could go across country like a comet'.

Romford, it will be recalled, was the only man to get the better of Sponge in the earlier book, causing his victim to reflect after a night spent in his squalid lodgings, 'this is the worst spec I ever made in my life. Fed on pork, fluted deaf, bit with bugs, and robbed at cards—fairly, downrightly robbed. Never was a more reg'ler plant put on a man . . .'[3]

Surtees now developed the portrait of Facey and like Sponge he was a strong enough character to hold together the whole flow of picaresque adventure which Young Tom Hall, Billy Pringle and Mr Bunting conspicuously were not. Facey, too, with all his faults, for he is a pretty thoroughgoing scoundrel, is a man robust enough in his misdoings to create his own appeal, whereas the other poor creatures could inspire only derision. As for Lucy (Mr Sponge absconds to Australia at the beginning of the book leaving Facey to take her up), she plays a far greater part than in *Mr Sponge* and becomes ever more resourceful and bewitching as the story unfolds.

The precise relationship between Facey and Lucy is never defined for Surtees skims adroitly over the thin ice of Victorian prudery in relating their joint and joyful career of horse-coping, hunting hounds together on other people's money from other people's houses, roguery, rascality, deceit, and deception—and sheer dishonest fun.

Facey himself is more than a little worried about what part the proprieties will play in interrupting their escapades and indeed, with the Heavyside Hounds, the first pack they bamboozle into accepting them, Lucy's prowess across coun-try on a screw Facey had had returned to him by a leading lady member as unfit to be a lady's mount, leads to unpleasant questions being asked:

'What! they were to have pretty horse-breakers down in the country, were they?' the ladies exclaimed. . . . 'They would have no impropriety! . . .' The 'H.H.' had always been a most respectable, well-conducted hunt; and respectable it should be to the end of the chapter or their husbands should have nothing to do with it. . . . 'No pretty horse-breaker!' was the cry.

Chapter 17

Next Surtees sails even closer to the wind for when, by another piece of chicanery, Facey takes the Larkspur Hounds, he and Lucy set up house together in Beldon Hall, Lucy masquerading as his step-sister 'Mrs Somerville', the widow of 'an Indian officer'. The pair are chaperoned—if it could be called that—by Lucy's mother (formerly a stage dresser) who also takes a false but apparently respectable name. Even so she has 'none of the self-possession of her elegant daughter' and is mistaken for her lady's maid on arrival at the local station.

Both Facey and Lucy are superlative riders across a country and Facey is, in addition, a huntsman of exceptional flair and skill so it is not surprising that the hunting scenes, especially when they are both taking on an awkward fence or Facey is puzzling out a line, are amongst the best that Surtees ever wrote.

There is a whole range of splendid subsidiary characters: Lord Lonergan and his son, the Honourable Lovetin Lonergan, Captain Spurrier the crack rider who is losing his nerve:

A strong tinge of hoar frost had shot across his once dark brown whiskers, and hardish falls had somewhat quenched the love of leaping. Still, men don't like admitting they are not so good as they have been, and persevere in the hopes that it is only a temporary depression from which they will speedily rally . . . Happy are they who go out to please themselves and not to astonish the others.

How true it all is! And Surtees, knowing his own nerve was failing, must have written those lines straight from his heart. Best of all of the minor characters is Miss Betsy Shannon, actress, singer, dancer, and model, whom Lucy out of the kindness of her heart asks down to stay at Beldon Hall. For the sake of her excursion into society she changes her name to the more aristocratic one of Miss Hamilton Howard to fit in with those newly acquired by her host and hostess. Ever alert to point up social sham Surtees comments:

'Betsy Shannon! What a name!' people would have said. 'What sort of people can those Romfords be to associate with such a person.' Then her manners, though not offensive, were rather forward, particularly with gentlemen; and altogether she required a little toning down. This, then, she had in the much coveted name of Howard; for what would have been downright vulgarity in a Shannon, became the easy manners of high life with a Howard.

Chapter 59

But it is Facey and more importantly, Lucy, who make the book. The reader cannot help but be captivated by her and his sympathies are fully engaged when she is finally unmasked by her former friend, once Lady Scattercash, now the Countess of Caperington, reformed character and atrocious snob—'You are Mrs Sponge—Lucy Glitters that was—most pernicious woman!'

No one knows from what recesses in mind or memory in Surtees Lucy Glitters sprang, for of Surtees's emotional life or the part women played in it we are told nothing. He wrote his wife a daily letter when separated from her but this may imply either lifelong devotion or the dutiful observance of a conscientious man. Everything in his writings implies that he neither liked, understood, nor had sympathy with women as a sex especially those of his own class to whom he conceded nothing in the way of fine feelings, tenderness, affection, or love—a word which is never mentioned throughout the whole canon of his work. The only members of the opposite sex to emerge from the books with any credit at all are Lucy, together with her friend Betsy Shannon, and perhaps Belinda, Charley Stobbs's betrothed, who really scarcely makes an impact as a character at all.

Mrs Jorrocks is a harridan, Mrs Pringle a cynical schemer, Jawleyford's daughters do not care much whom they catch so long as that someone *is* a catch, Major Yammerton's are much the same, Angelena Blunt is a heartless flirt with her eye on the main chance though at least her skill and grace on a horse are conceded her.

They all, too, with the exception of Lucy Glitters, share the fact that the men in their lives have only one function—to provide. Surtees's women and indeed his men, too, know nothing of sexual desires or urges; they have no existence below the waist. This ignoring or suppression of one of the most basic and important of all human instincts was, of course, endemic in Victorian fiction. Thackeray, who had had his share of sexual encounters, recognized this and railed against it in a famous passage: 'Since the author of *Tom Jones* was buried, no writer of fiction among us has been permitted to depict to his utmost power a MAN. We must drape him and give him a certain conventional simper. Society will not tolerate the natural in our art.'

Trollope, too, though he never put it as bluntly as Thackeray, recognized this loss and handicap. Michael Sadleir, the first of his biographers to interpret him for modern readers, explains his attitude to it in this way:

To murders and forgeries may be added—if one is agog for crime—adulteries and bigamies . . . but because a large part of social wisdom is restraint, alike of gesture and of word, his books are restrained—not in incident or necessarily in emotion—but in expression. He writes adult books for adult people. But because he writes in terms of polite society, because he is in the truest sense a 'man of the world', he is too civilised and too experienced to forget the social decencies for the sake of the social sins.[4]

The fact remains that though it is sublimated, his characters, especially in the Palliser novels, are driven and harried by sexual desire.

With Surtees one can only speculate on the reasons for his savagery towards women of his own class or those such as Mrs Pringle and the Countess of Caperington who aspired to attain it, and his tenderness towards those of the *demi-monde*.

Did he stress the bitchiness of respectable women because he believed it came from the suppression of their natural desires and contrasted this with the easiness and charm of their fallen sisters who by satisfying them had set themselves free? Was he simply using this gallery of respectable and detestable women to express his loathing of primness and pretension? It may be, of course, that he saw in the double standard in sexual matters then pertaining a flagrant example of the hypocrisy he so hated, but even this does not really explain the persistent cynicism and satire which infused his portraits of 'match-making mothers and blushing virgins'.

Certainly Surtees must have been aware of the role sex played in the lives of men and women—especially men—as anyone would have been who had lived his youth in a London just emerging from Regency licence, where 'fair cyprians' and 'pretty horse-breakers' had a society and standing of their own, where sex was flaunted and exploited and child prostitution flourished. That he preferred these honest purveyors of their sexual attractions, with their experience and understanding of the other sex and their ability to cosset a man and make him comfortable and happy, to their proud and prim sisters, whose payment was extracted not in coin but in bondage, is apparent from his writings. Convention prevented him from expressing this preference openly until in *Mr Facey Romford's Hounds,* written when old age was pressing upon him, he took convention by the throat and threw it as far away as he could. He was too explicit for certain mid-Victorians. And, even more heinous in their eyes, he failed to point a moral. For when 'the bubble burst' as he put it, and the illicit pair were unmasked, nemesis did not descend upon them. Lucy, who hears that Sponge has prospered greatly in Australia, sets out to join him. The voyage out agrees with her and she arrives 'looking, if possible, handsomer than ever' and she and Sponge are reunited.

Facey, too, falls on his feet. After his exposure as an impostor he still has 'assurance enough for anything. He could kill a fox with anyone and had as good a pack of hounds as ever came into a country', and since 'nothing pleases people so much as a dashing fearless rider', he continues to hunt the country until he marries and he too emigrates to Australia to look after his wife's expectations there. In Melbourne he runs into Sponge and they agree to set up a bank under the name and style of 'Romford and Sponge'. The very last sentence of this most reprehensible tale is Surtees's own comment: 'Good luck attend their exertions, say we!'

So Surtees, in what was to be his final book, cocked a snook at Victorian respectability, indeed at all that those who laid down the guidelines for Victorian fiction thought right and proper. There was no moral to be drawn from this tale. Virtue did not emerge triumphant and, more reprehensibly, vice was not suitably punished. No wonder that Trollope, a moralist at heart for all his sophistication, disapproved of him and that Thackeray, who shared some of Surtees's cynicism, read his books with relish.

While he was working on the book Surtees approached Mr Evans of Bradbury and Evans with a view to arranging publication in monthly parts. Evans, however, was slow to give any assurances or to enter into any contract until he was certain of having Leech's illustrations. But Leech was, as usual, 'overwhelmed with work' as he told Surtees in reply to his letter asking him to accept the task. It was unfortunate for Surtees that the writing of *Facey* coincided with Leech's ill-advised experiment in oil-painting. Assisted by technical advice from Millais he was just then busy selecting certain of his *Punch* sketches for enlargement and adaptation into oils. This was effected by an ingenious india-rubber block which, having been first impressed on the sketches, enlarged itself and thus enabled him to transfer them to canvas. The result was then coloured in oils by the artist. In the opinion of almost every critic then and since the pictures produced by this process were devoid of merit, for Leech's genius lay in the sketch and the miniature.

But Leech, who had hitherto scorned oils for reasons known only to himself, persisted in the venture and such was his

'Billy is introduced to the Major's Harriers'

John Leech illustration for *Ask Mamma*, 1858

'The Hunt Ball - "Ask Mamma" Polka'

John Leech illustration for *Ask Mamma*, 1858

Hamsterley Hall, Co. Durham. From an engraving

Surtees in old age. Portrait by G. D. Armour

reputation that he succeeded in holding an exhibition of sixty-seven of these paintings in the Egyptian Hall in London. His friend and benefactor Thackeray wrote an enthusiastic notice of the exhibition in *The Times* and, it is believed, due to this and no other cause, the exhibition's financial, if not critical success was assured. When it closed Leech had netted no less than £6,000 which at the time he badly needed. But the work and worry entailed in this enterprise caused a further degeneration in his health. His insomnia increased as did a curious and violent allergy to noise from which he had been suffering for some years. Despite Surtees's letters which, at first propitiatory, became almost imploring as they elicited no response, there was little chance of his undertaking the work on *Facey* and shortly afterwards he left for an extended Continental tour in an effort to restore his shattered health.

Evans was still determined not to publish without Leech as an illustrator so Surtees offered the book to *The Field* as a serial. *The Field,* however, declined it. Surtees remained convinced, and rightly so, that it was his best work since *Sponge,* and would repeat that book's success.

Then both Leech and he suffered a further blow, for on 24 December 1863 their great friend Thackerary was found dead in bed. They exchanged letters of mutual condolence. 'I was much shocked at the death of poor Thackeray,' Surtees wrote, 'to my mind by far the foremost writer of his age.' 'His loss to me is a loss indeed,' Leech wrote back, and here he spoke truly for Thackeray had set him on the path to success and had never ceased to help and befriend him.

Thackeray's death and the grief it caused Leech meant even further delays, and Surtees's letters continued in the same imploring tone very unlike the arrogant and terse communications he had heretofore addressed to editors and illustrators:

MY DEAR LEECH,—Greetings. Do you think there is any chance of our getting together again in the way of work? I was in hopes 'Romford' would have made his appearance next month but as yet I have no prelude in the shape of a prospectus. I should much like if we could finish together. How say you, John Leech, shall it be a go or not?[5]

But, do what he would, Leech continued to procrastinate.

Surtees had, too, at this time, other things to worry him and to claim his attention. The promoters of the Derwent Valley Railway were proposing to drive the branch line from Newcastle to Consett across his Hamsterley property, cutting it in two. Not only that but their plan involved the construction of two great viaducts, one consisting of ten arches 120 feet high to be situated only half a mile from the Hall itself. The despoliation of his property and invasion of his privacy must have been a sore affront to this most property-conscious and private of men, and he determined to resist the scheme with every means in his power. 'I don't want the railway which cuts me most desperately to waste', he wrote, and from his position in the country and as a prominent landowner he exercised what influence he could against it, raising local agitation and lobbying members of Parliament. Despite all he could do he was fighting a losing battle. The promoters secured the passing of an act giving them the right to do as they desired. Both the law and the march of progress (two things he detested equally) were against him. The plans went ahead and Surtees's own lawyers' assurances that the siting of the line would benefit his colliery interests totally failed to placate him.

But at least publication of *Facey* seemed within sight at last, for Leech finally gave word that he would start work on the illustrations, though even then he dragged his feet. 'I had fully intended commencing in February, but found it impossible. However I will have a shy at it for March if you do not think it is too late . . .' '*March* be it, if you please,' Surtees wrote back, a note of tartness for once coming into his correspondence with the artist.[6]

March, in the end, it was. Although Surtees appears to have had no warning or premonition of it, he had, in fact, very little longer to live. In the event he did not see even the publication of the first of the monthly parts which contained much of Leech's finest work. So unaware was Surtees of the approaching end that he was during this time making notes for his autobiography which, astonishingly enough, he had decided would be published under his own name. In *Hawbuck Grange* he had stated catagorically: 'We may say with our excellent friend Peter Morris [one of Lockhart's pseudonyms] that if putting our Christian name and surname at the beginning of a book were necessary conditions to the dignity of authorship, we should never be one while we live.' This may imply that he intended the autobiography to be published posthumously, but if so this is not apparent from the notes, to which he had given the preliminary title of *Sporting and Social Recollections.*

This work had not progressed very far when the weather closed in. There was no prospect of hunting for some time and to escape the bitter cold ('Yours truly but three-quarters frozen', he ended his last letter to Leech), he and Mrs Surtees decided to journey south to Brighton. They stayed as they were accustomed to at Mutton's Hotel in the King's Road. During the night of 16 March Surtees awoke complaining of pains in his chest. In ten minutes he was dead. He was in his fifty-ninth year. His body was taken north and he was buried as he would have liked, privately, with the minimum of fuss, in Elchester churchyard, hard by his beloved Hamsterley.

Surtees's essential characteristics had hardly altered in the course of his life. Tetchy and cantankerous at times, he was dutiful as a public servant, impartial as a magistrate and legislator, a worthy husband, and a doughty fighter for those of the oppressed whose causes he considered just. He was not a great writer but at times he touched the fringe of greatness and he had at least one quality all great writers must possess: he could create a world of his own and people it with characters vibrant with life. Monsters they may be, but most of them can still be met with in sporting or social circles if one looks about one. He had his own vision of the world; it was a narrow one but he was true to it. There is neither sentiment nor subtlety in him; his view of human nature was base; just

185

as he had no time for pomp or pretentiousness so neither kindness, affection, nor love enter into the world in which his characters move. These are grave defects but at least we know where we are with him. He is a caricaturist, a Rowlandson of fiction, and his caricatures are based on a merciless and accurate observation of what he took to be the truth of human nature.

Kipling, in one of his best and strangely neglected short stories, *My Son's Wife,* has provided perhaps the truest summing up of the world created and brought alive by Surtees. Midmore, the London aesthete, a dedicated member of 'the Immoderate left', on inheriting a small country estate is driven by lack of reading matter on the shelves of his house to take down and 'paw over a few score books in a panelled room called the library'.

It was a foul world into which he peeped for the first time—a heavy-eating, hard-drinking hell of horse-copers, swindlers, match-making mothers, economically dependent virgins selling themselves blushingly for cash and lands; Jews, tradesmen, and an ill-considered spawn of Dickens-and-horsedung characters (I give Midmore's own criticism), but he read on, fascinated, and behold, from the pages leaped, as it were, the brother to the red-eyed man of the brook, bellowing at a landlord (here Midmore realised that *he* was that very animal) for new barns; and another man who, like himself again, objected to hoof-marks on gravel. Outrageous as thought and conception were, the stuff seemed to have the rudiments of observation. He dug out other volumes....[7]

Meanwhile Leech was facing up to his own end: 'I shall not long survive him,' he said to his wife on hearing of Thackeray's death. He did not live to complete the illustrations for *Facey Romford,* and he died some seven months after the death of Surtees on 26 October 1864, at the early age of forty-seven. During his lifetime, for *Punch* alone he had executed 3,000 drawings of which 600 were cartoons. For this work he had received no less than £40,000 but he did not die in affluence for, like many of his kind, he was feckless, over-generous, and a bad manager of money.

Shortly before his death Messrs. Agnew had offered Leech £1,000 for four pictures. Badly in need of money as ever it seemed to him to be a chance of salvation. On the day he died he said to his wife, 'Please God, Annie, I shall make a fortune yet'. It was not to be, and he died poor. He was incomparably the greatest sporting illustrator of his time. The few final plates required for *Facey* were supplied by Phiz, but they are wooden compared to Leech's work.

After their deaths the reputations and sales of most authors show a sharp decline. By a paradox which would have appealed to his cynical nature Surtees's posthumous reputation grew. Although no obituaries appeared in either the national or, astonishingly, the local papers, almost immediately a cult began to grow around him. Naturally enough this was led by the sporting set who did, however, form a far greater proportion of the reading public then than now. Soon the sayings of Jorrocks passed into the hunting man's vocabulary until they became practically part of the language, and the counterparts of the characters who thronged *Mr Sponge* and *Facey Romford* began to be recognized amongst the followers of every hunt in the kingdom. This latter intimation of immortality has persisted until this day. Kipling made Midmore, the aesthete, use the books as a *Sortes Surteesianae* to identify the characters whom he saw about him, and Sassoon declared that every follower of the Ringwell Hunt had stepped straight out of his pages.

Surtees's popularity grew, too, with the progress of the Industrial Revolution, for the newly enriched who were setting themselves up as country gentlemen were only too glad to laugh at the shocking exploits of his anti-heroes and to enjoy the savage caricatures of those aristocrats or earlier *arrivistes* who had snubbed or sneered at them in their upward climb. His work became fashionable to such an extent that before long the editor of *The Field* had to publish a notice to contributors asking them to refrain from quoting Jorrocks—'for reasons of space'!

Gradually, he won a wider notice and recognition though

the critics still largely ignored him or, if they dealt with him at all, did so disparagingly or inaccurately. Even as late as 1947 such scrupulous bibliographers as John Carter and Michael Sadleir were recording him as the author of *Mr Jorrocks's Sporting Tours,* thus collating two fine books under one confused title. The taint of 'coarseness', too, was laid upon him until well into the twentieth century and E.Œ. Somerville, writing in the *New Statesman* (of all places) allowed herself to wonder 'If, at that time, all men were pretentious, tippling and cowardly, all women spiteful, vulgar and affected...' Other more discerning eyes appreciated Surtees's worth. Someone who was admired by Tennyson, Thackeray, and William Morris in his own day, by Kipling, Arnold Bennett ('Many thanks for putting me right on Surtees,' he wrote to Sassoon, *'Facey Romford* is the real thing'), Sassoon himself and Orwell cannot be as lightly dismissed as his detractors would wish. More recently Walter Allen, in his survey of the English novel, has granted that 'Of the richness of his humour there can be no doubt and Jorrocks and Pigg, the huntsman, though minor immortals are immortals none the less.'[8] Sir Victor Pritchett, too, has devoted a perceptive essay to him.

Too much cannot be claimed for him. That his range and his talent were limited and his control of his medium too haphazard cannot be denied. But that as a social historian of his time, with his detailed descriptions of the manners, morals, meals, and dress of his characters, he was unrivalled is equally undeniable. It is also true to say that with his insight into the social and sporting personalities and life of his day, illuminated as it was on occasion with flashes of comic genius, he is unique. And the gallery of grotesques which he created, headed by Jorrocks J., each of whom had his feet on a foundation of truth, is impressive by any standards: Lord Scamperdale, Jack Spraggon, that 'fine natural blackguard', Cuddy Flintoff the *faux* sportsman, Sir Moses Mainchance, Lord Heartycheer the snob, Jawleyford, Johnny O'Dicey the sharp—one could continue with the catalogue almost *ad infinitum* and every one of them is in his own way alive and convincing. Best of all, of course, are those two hard riders Mr Sponge and Facey Romford, together with their foil, the beautiful and 'tolerably virtuous' Lucy Glitters. Had he known that these three are still crossing the country in the hearts of sportsmen the world over more than a hundred years after his death, and that Mr Jorrocks's 'lectors' are still enchanting them, he would have asked no more, save perhaps to have heard Thackeray repeat the remark he made on reading the draft of the last posthumous book, that he would have given all he had to have written *Mr Facey Romford's Hounds*.

Select Bibliography

All works listed below were published in London unless otherwise stated.

Apperley, C.J. ('Nimrod'), *The Life of A Sportsman* (1842)

——*Memoirs of the Life of John Mytton* (1837)

——*The Chace, The Road and The Turf,* with an introduction by John Sparrow (1927)

——*My Life and Times,* edited with additions by E.D. Cuming (Edinburgh and London, 1927)

Blew, C.W.A., *A History of Steeplechasing* (1901)

Bovill, E.W., *The England of Nimrod and Surtees 1815–1854* (Oxford, 1959)

Carey, John, *Thackeray, Prodigal Genius* (1977)

Carr, Raymond, *English Fox-Hunting* (1976)

Carter, John and Sadleir, Michael, *A Catalogue of Victorian Fiction* (Cambridge, 1947)

Cooper, Leonard, *R.S. Surtees* (1952)

Cuming, E.D., *R.S. Surtees, Creator of Jorrocks,* by Himself and E.D. Cuming (1924)

——'*Handley Cross* behind the Scenes' *(Blackwood's Magazine,* Oct. 1924)

Darton, H., *From Surtees to Sassoon* (n.d.)

Day, J. Wentworth, *Inns of Sport* (1949)

de Broke, Lord Willoughby, *The Sport of Our Ancestors* (1921)

Drinkwater, John (ed.), *The Eighteen-Sixties* (1932)

Edwards, Lionel, *Thy Servant the Horse* (1952)

Frederick, Sir Charles (ed.), *Foxhunting* (n.d.)

Frith, William Powell, *John Leech, His Life and Work,* 2 vols. (1891)

Gough, Lionel, *Hunting Scenes from Surtees* (1953)

Higginson, A. Henry, *British and American Sporting Authors* (1951)

Kirby, C., *The English Country Gentleman* (n.d.)

McCausland, Hugh, *Old Sporting* (1948)

Noakes, Aubrey, *The World of Henry Alken* (1952)

——*Horses, Hounds and Humans* (1957)

191

Select Bibliography

Paget, Guy, *The Sporting Pictures of England* (1935)

Price, R.G.G., *A History of Punch* (1957)

Ray, Cyril, *Surtees, Scenes and Characters* (1949)

Rose, June, *The Drawings of John Leech* (1950)

Rose, R.N., *The Field, 1853–1953* (1953)

Sparrow, W. Shaw, *British Sporting Prints* (1922)

Steel, Anthony, *Jorrocks's England* (1932)

Surtees, Robert Smith, *The Horseman's Manual* (1831)

——*Jorrocks's Jaunts and Jollities* (1838)

——*Handley Cross* (1843)

——*Hillingdon Hall* (1845)

——*The Analysis of the Hunting Field* (1846)

——*Hawbuck Grange* (1847)

——*Mr Sponge's Sporting Tour* (1853)

——*Hints to Railway Travellers and Country Visitors to London* (1852)

——*Ask Mamma* (1858)

——*Plain or Ringlets?* (1860)

——*Mr Facey Romford's Hounds* (1865)

——*Young Tom Hall* (1926)

——*The Hunting Tours of Surtees,* ed. E. D. Cuming, reprinted from the *New Sporting Magazine* (1927)

——*Town and Country Papers,* ed. E. D. Cuming (1929)

——*The Life and Writings of Nimrod* by the Author of Handley Cross *(Ainsworth's Magazine, 1845–6)*

'Thormandy', *Kings of the Hunting Field* (1899)

Watson, Frederick, *Robert Smith Surtees. A Critical Study* (1933)

Whyte-Melville, G.J., *Digby Grand* (1853)

——*Market Harborough* (1861)

References

CHAPTER ONE: Opening Days
1. Frederick Watson, *Robert Smith Surtees. A Critical Study* (1933), p. 86
2. *R. S. Surtees, Creator of Jorrocks*, by Himself and E. D. Cuming (1924), p. 192
3. Ibid., p. 7
4. Ibid., p. 13

CHAPTER TWO: Brighton and Boulogne
1. *R. S. Surtees*, op. cit., p. 17
2. Ibid., p. 29
3. Ibid., p. 31
4. *Mr. Sponge's Sporting Tour*, ch. 31
5. *R. S. Surtees*, op. cit., p. 35
6. Ibid., p. 47 *et seq.*
7. Ibid., p. 55

CHAPTER THREE: Nimrod
1. 'A Notice of Nimrod' by 'HC' in 4th edn. of Nimrod's *Life of Mytton*
2. Ibid.
3. Ibid.
4. Ibid.
5. *The Life and Writings of Nimrod* by the Author of Handley Cross (1845–6)
6. Frederick Watson, op. cit., p. 59
7. 'A Notice of Nimrod', op. cit.
8. Ibid.
9. Nimrod, *My Life and Times,* with additions by E. D. Cuming (1927)
10. *The Life and Writings of Nimrod*, op. cit.
11. Ibid.
12. Ibid.

CHAPTER FOUR: Journalist and Editor

1. *Town and Country Papers,* Part 8, ch. 4
2. Nimrod, *The Life of a Sportsman* (1842)
3. *Town and Country Papers*
4. *R. S. Surtees,* op. cit., p. 62
5. Ibid., p. 118
6. Ibid., p. 72
7. Ibid., p. 65
8. Ibid., p. 64
9. *The Life and Writings of Nimrod,* op. cit.
10. Hesketh Pearson, *Walter Scott, his Life and Work* (1954)
11. *R. S. Surtees,* op. cit., p. 25
12. See *R. S. Surtees,* op. cit.
13. Ibid., p. 134

CHAPTER FIVE: *Jaunts and Jollities* and the End of Editing

1. *R. S. Surtees,* op. cit., p. 113
2. *R. S. Surtees,* op. cit., p. 113
3. *The Life and Writings of Nimrod,* op. cit.
4. Ibid.
5. 'Our Visit to Nimrod' by the Author of *Handley Cross, New Sporting Magazine,* Vol. 3
6. *The Life and Writings of Nimrod,* op. cit.
7. 'A Notice of Nimrod', op. cit.
8. *R. S. Surtees,* op. cit., p. 97
9. 'Nimrod's Northern Tour' in *New Sporting Magazine,* 1838
10. *The Life and Writings of Nimrod,* op. cit.
11. *R. S. Surtees,* op. cit., p. 85
12. Ibid., p. 211
13. *New Sporting Magazine,* Dec. 1836
14. *R. S. Surtees,* op. cit., p. 147
15. Ibid., p. 148
16. *R. S. Surtees,* op. cit., p. 156

CHAPTER SIX: Jorrocks

1. *The Life and Writings of Nimrod,* op. cit.
2. *New Sporting Magazine,* Jan. 1839
3. *The Life and Writings of Nimrod,* op. cit.
4. *R. S. Surtees,* op. cit., p. 200

5. Ibid., p. 201
6. Ibid., p. 214
7. E. D. Cuming, *'Handley Cross* behind the Scenes', *Blackwood's Magazine*, Oct. 1924
8. Ibid.
9. G. K. Chesterton, Introduction to *The Pickwick Papers* (1959)
10. E. D. Cuming, op. cit.
11. Ibid.
12. *R. S. Surtees*, op. cit., p. 219
13. *Quarterly Review*, Vol. 71
14. Nimrod, *My Life and Times*, p. 312 *et seq.*
15. E. D. Cuming, op. cit.

CHAPTER SEVEN: The Failure of *Handley Cross*

1. *R. S. Surtees*, op. cit., p. 86
2. *Handley Cross*, ch. 32
3. Ibid., ch. 28
4. *Hillingdon Hall*, ch. 11
5. Victor Bonham Carter, 'Authors by Profession' (Society of Authors, 1978)
6. *Handley Cross*, ch. 32
7. *Young Tom Hall*, ch. 15
8. *R. S. Surtees*, op. cit., p. 227

CHAPTER EIGHT: Hack-work and *Hawbuck Grange*

1. *The Analysis of the Hunting Field*, ch. 10
2. Ibid., ch. 3
3. Ibid., ch. 2
4. Ibid., ch. 18
5. *R. S. Surtees*, op. cit., p. 144
6. *Hawbuck Grange*, ch. 2
7. *R. S. Surtees*, op. cit., p. 234
8. Ibid., p. 242
9. 'A Notice of Nimrod', op. cit.
10. *R. S. Surtees*, op. cit., pp. 236–7

CHAPTER NINE: *Mr Sponge's Sporting Tour*

1. *Mr Sponge's Sporting Tour*, ch. 1
2. *R. S. Surtees*, op. cit., p. 260

3. *Mr Sponge's Sporting Tour*, ch. 71
4. *R. S. Surtees*, op. cit., p. 247
5. Ibid., p. 245
6. William Powell Frith, *John Leech, His Life and Work* (2 vols., 1891), Vol. 2, ch. 4
7. Ibid.
8. *New Sporting Magazine*, Jan. 1853
9. *R. S. Surtees*, op. cit., p. 263

CHAPTER TEN: *Young Tom Hall*

1. *R. S. Surtees*, op. cit., p. 277
2. Ibid., p. 274
3. E. D. Cuming, Introduction to *Young Tom Hall* (1926)
4. Frederick Watson, op. cit., p. 241
5. *Young Tom Hall*, ch. 18
6. E. D. Cuming, Introduction to *YTH*

CHAPTER ELEVEN: Jorrocks Redivivus

1. *R. S. Surtees*, op. cit., p. 273
2. June Rose, *The Drawings of John Leech* (1950)
3. Virginia Woolf, *The Common Reader* (1932), Vol. 2
4. *New Sporting Magazine*, March 1855
5. Ibid., April 1855
6. Frederick Watson, op. cit., pp. 242–3
7. E. D. Cuming, '*Handley Cross* behind the Scenes'

CHAPTER TWELVE: *The Field*

1. R. S. Surtees, op. cit., p. 273
2. Ibid., p. 293
3. R. N. Rose, *The Field* (1953), ch. 1
4. Ibid.
5. *R. S. Surtees*, op. cit. pp. 296–7
6. R. N. Rose, op. cit., ch. 3
7. Ibid.
8. *R. S. Surtees*, op. cit. p. 300
9. R. N. Rose, op. cit., ch. 6

CHAPTER THIRTEEN: *Ask Mamma*

1. *R. S. Surtees*, op. cit., p. 327
2. *Ask Mamma*, ch. 39
3. *R. S. Surtees*, op. cit., p. 308

References

CHAPTER FOURTEEN: Gone to Ground

1. *R. S. Surtees,* op. cit., p. 159
2. Ibid., pp. 307 and 309
3. *Mr Sponge's Sporting Tour*, ch. 63
4. Michael Sadleir, *Trollope: A Commentary* (1972)
5. *R. S. Surtees,* op. cit., pp. 319–20
6. Ibid., p. 320
7. Rudyard Kipling, *My Son's Wife* from *A Diversity of Creatures* (1917)
8. Walter Allen, *The English Novel* (1954)

Index

Index

Cotton, Sir St Vincent, 10, 23
County Durham Conservative
  Association, 116
Cox, E.W., 163
'Craven', *see* Carleton, J.W.
Craven, Earl of, 37
Cresswell, Sackville, 15–17
Cruikshank, George, 135
Cuming, E.D., 80, 89, 96, 148, 160

'Dashwood', *see* Copland
'Day with the Surrey, A', 60
Derwent and Shotley Bridge
  Agricultural Society, 141
Derwent Valley Railway, 184
Dickens, Charles, 9, 90, 101, 137–8,
  142–3
Dictionary of National Biography, 80, 109,
  151
Dowling, Vincent George, 158
Drinkwater, John, 151
Durham: Surtees's study on, 174–5
Durham Grammar School, 3–5

Elcho, Lord, 140, 142, 158
Eld, Captain, 11–12
Encyclopaedia Britannica, 65
Encyclopaedia of Rural Sports (Blaine),
  164–5
Evans (of Bradbury and Evans), 182–3

Fenwick, Addison, 95
Field, The, 158–63, 183, 187
Forester, Squire, 131
Fortescue, John, 151
France, 13–21, 96
Fraser's Magazine, 65
Freeman, Captain, 109
Frith, William Powell, 137–8, 151

Gablenz, Baron, 13, 125, 173
Gomm (of Bedford Hotel,
  Leamington), 73–4
Grand National Hunt Committee, 134
Grant, Sir Francis, 48–9, 88
Greville, Charles, 88–9

Hamsterley Hall (Co. Durham):
  Surtees's home at, 1, 4, 74–5;
  Nimrod visits, 75–6; Surtees inherits,
  87, 116; railway traverses, 184
Handley Cross: legal life in, 7; on
  hunting thrills, 12; on London, 25;

humour, 44, 115; characters, 61, 65,
  90, 98; serialized, 80; writing and
  publication, 90–1, 93–4, 97, 103;
  plot, 101; lacks illustrations, 103–4,
  108; reviewed, 104–5, 153–6; Nimrod
  challenges Surtees over, 106–7;
  coarseness in, 110; failure, 110-11,
  149, 157; soldiers in, 116; reissued
  with Leech illustrations, 121, 149–53,
  157; *see also* Jorrocks, John
Hart-Davis, Sir Rupert, 171*n*
Hawbuck Grange, 13, 102, 121–6, 136
Hawker, Col. Peter, 50–1
Heath, Henry, 115
Herbert, Sir Alan P., 171*n*
Herring, J.F., 49
Higgs, Phoebe, 131
Hill, Matthew Davenport, 74
Hillingdon Hall, 96, 112–15
Hinde, John Hodgson, 86–7, 106
Hinde, Richard, 87
Hinkley (Leicestershire), 23, 25
Hints to Railway Travellers, 41
Hogg, James ('the Ettrick Shepherd'),
  51, 70
Hood, Thomas, 97
Horlock, W.H. ('Scrutator'), 139
Horseman's Manual, The, 21, 46

Jews, 168, 172
Jorrocks, John (*character*): on hunting,
  4; and London, 7–8, 25; identity of,
  8, 80; on horsemanship, 12; and
  bagman, 18; on coaching, 39; on
  eagle-eye view, 43; development of
  character, 59, 60–3, 79–80, 89–90,
  100, 102, 109–13; on Nimrod, 64;
  insanity, 65, 91, 94; serialized, 80; on
  huntsman's cares, 87; as magistrate,
  95–6, 113; and Ego, 97–8, 102; social
  position, 108; as MP, 113; grows old,
  114; on soldiers, 116; Leech depicts,
  149–51; on fox, 171; reputation as
  literary character, 187–8
Jorrocks's Jaunts and Jollities: on
  coaching, 39; and character of
  Jorrocks, 60, 62–4; on city interests,
  63; 2nd edition fails, 78–9, 112; first
  published, 89; Ackermann acquires
  rights to, 99; illustrations, 103

Kintore, Lord, 75
Kipling, Rudyard, 152, 169, 186–8

200